Math Trailblazers®

Fourth Edition

Common Core State Standards

Student Activity Book

Volume 1

Kendall Hunt

A TIMS® CURRICULUM
University of Illinois at Chicago

Math Trailblazers®

Dedication

This book is dedicated to the children and teachers who let us see the magic in their classrooms and to our families who wholeheartedly supported us while we searched for ways to make it happen.

The TIMS Project

In memory of Philip Wagreich,
our visionary, mentor, leader, and friend.

UIC UNIVERSITY OF ILLINOIS AT CHICAGO

The original edition was based on work supported by the National Science Foundation under grant No. MDR 9050226 and the University of Illinois at Chicago. The current material is based on work supported by the National Science Foundation under award No. 0242704. Any opinions, findings, and conclusions or recommendations expressed in this publication are those of the authors and do not necessarily reflect the views of the granting agencies.

Production Date: July 9, 2014
Printed by: Webcrafters, Inc.

United States of America
Batch number: 43243602

Table of Contents

Unit 3: Exploring Multiplication 81

Unit 4: Place Value Concepts 95

Unit 5: Area of Different Shapes 133

Unit 7: Subtracting Larger Numbers............................215

Unit 1

Sampling and Classifying

Math Facts
Use the practice in this unit to review the addition facts.

Name _____

Date _____

First Names Data Table and Graph

Complete the table. Use the table to make a bar graph.

Frequency of Letters in First Name

L Number of Letters	S Number of Students
1	
2	
3	
4	
5	
6	
7	
8	
9	
10	
11	

Frequency of Letters in First Name

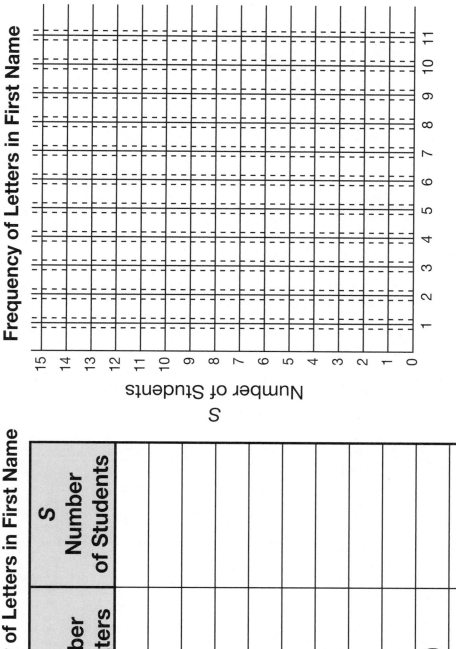

Family Names Data Table

Homework

Collect at least ten first names from your family. Count the number of letters in each name. Write each name in the corresponding row.

L Number of Letters in First Name	Names of Family Members
1	
2	
3	
4	
5	
6	
7	
8	
9	
10	
11	

Family Names Graph

Homework

Dear Family Member:

In class, we collected data on the number of letters in our first names. We displayed this data in a bar graph. Now, your child is using the data from your *Family Names Data Table* to create a new bar graph. Ask your child how this graph compares to the graph made in school.

Thank you for your help.

Graph the data from your *Family Names Data Table*. Use the dotted lines to help you draw the bars.

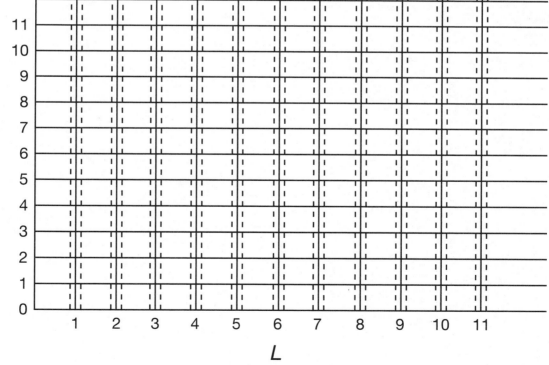

Family Names

Name _____

Date _____

Careless Professor Peabody

Professor Peabody lost his *First Names* data table. Use the graph to make a new data table.

Frequency of Letters in First Name

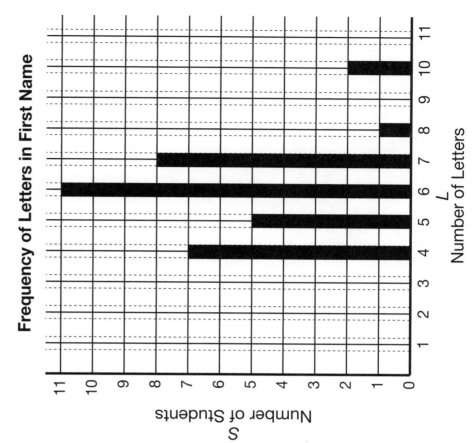

Frequency of Letters in First Name

L Number of Letters	*S* Number of Students
1	
2	
3	
4	
5	
6	
7	
8	
9	
10	
11	

Name _____ Date _____

Number Line Target Game

This game is for two players. The object of the game is to be the player that covers the sum equal to or greater than the target number.

I will cover an eight. Fifteen plus eight equals twenty-three.

Hmm. The target number is 30. 23 + 7 = 30. If I cover a seven, I will win!

Materials: • *Number Line Target Game Boards*   • game markers

Directions

1. Player 1 chooses a target number. Start with a small number, such as 20, and play on Game Board 1.

2. Player 1 covers a number and then Player 2 covers a number. Players track the sum of the covered numbers using the number line.

3. Take turns covering numbers. The winner covers the number that makes the sum equal to or greater than the target number.

Variation

Play the game using Game Board 2 with a larger target number, such as 100.

Number Line Target Game Boards

Game Board 1

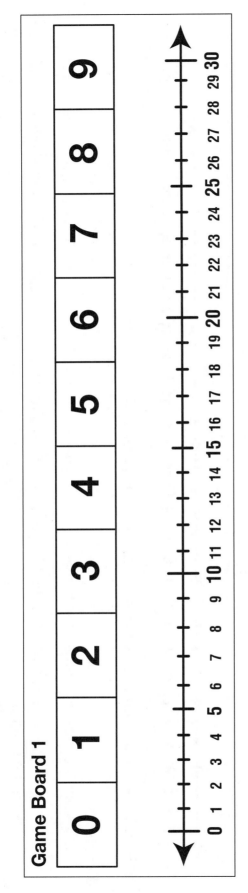

Game Board 2

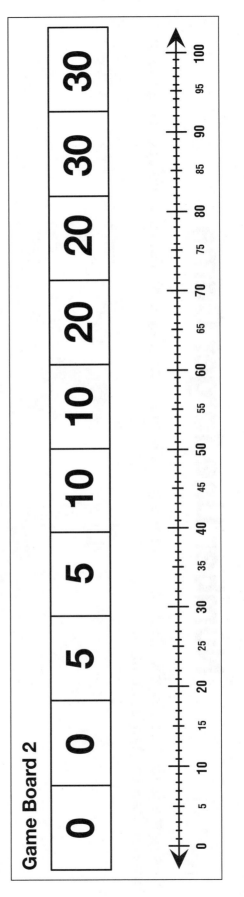

Kind of Bean Lab

Use the TIMS Laboratory Method to investigate the population of beans.

Draw a picture of the lab setup. Show the variables and the materials you will use.

1. What are the two main variables in your experiment?

_____ and _____

Collect the data. Use your scoop to take a sample from the container. Record the number of each kind of bean in the table.

Kind of Bean

K Kind of Bean	N Number of Beans Pulled

Graph

Make a bar graph of your results. Remember to label the graph.

Explore

Answer the following questions using your data table and graph.

2. A. What kind of bean is most common in your sample?

_____

B. How many do you have of this kind of bean? _____

3. A. What kind of bean is least common in your sample? _____

B. How many do you have of this kind of bean? _____

4. How many more of the most common beans do you have than the least common? Show or tell how you know.

5. What is the total number of beans in your sample? _____

6. Show or tell how you found the answer to Question 5.

A Second Sample

 ## Check-In: Questions 7–11

7. You are going to collect a second sample with the same size scoop.

A. Predict which kind of bean will be the most common.

_____

B. Predict which kind of bean will be the least common.

_____

C. Show or tell how you decided.

8. Collect a second sample with the same size scoop. Count the beans and record your data in the table.

Second Sample

K Kind of Bean	*N* Number of Beans Pulled

9. Graph your data.

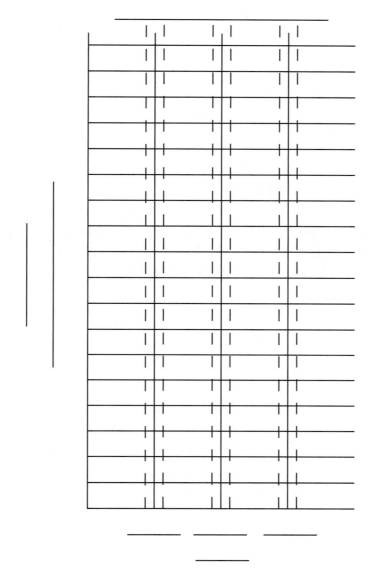

10. A. What kind of bean is most common in this sample?

_____

B. What kind of bean is least common in this sample?

_____

11. Were your predictions in Question 7 correct? Why or why not?

Population Predictions

12. Use your data to make predictions about the bean population (all of the beans in the class container). Predict which bean is the most common and which bean is the least common. Tell why you think so.

13. Suppose you use a much larger scoop to take a sample.

A. How will the data in your data table change?

B. How will your graph change?

Name _____ Date _____

Kind of Bean Lab
Check-In: Questions 7–11
Feedback Box

Expectation	Check In	Comments
Draw a scaled bar graph from a table. [Questions 8–9]	E2	
Read a table or scaled graph to find information about a data set. [Questions 10 A–B]	E3	
Make predictions and generalizations about a population from a sample using data tables and graphs. [Questions 7A–B and 11]	E4	

Yes . . .	Yes, but . . .	No, but . . .	No . . .

MPE5. Show my work.
I show or tell how I arrived at my answer so someone else can understand my thinking. [Question 7C]

Toni's Candy Grab

Homework

1. Toni filled a bag with red, green, and blue candy. She reached inside and took out a sample. Graph the data she wrote in the table.

- Title the graph.
- Label the axes.
- Scale the vertical axis.

Toni's Data

C Color	N Number of Candies Pulled
red	39
green	12
blue	5

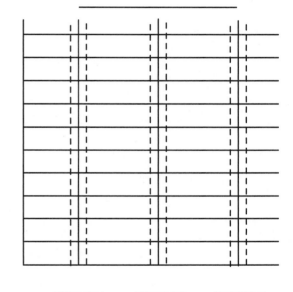

2. How many candies did she grab in her sample ?

_____

3. Toni reaches inside her bag again and pulls out only one candy. Use the words impossible, unlikely, likely, or certain to describe the following events:

   A. She pulls out a blue candy.   _____

   B. She pulls out a red candy.   _____

   C. She pulls out a piece of candy.   _____

   D. She pulls out a yellow candy.   _____

Picture Graphs

1. Linda's mom is a baker. Linda decided to use a picture graph to show the different flavors of cake her mother baked during a day. Linda finished her data table but forgot to finish the graph. Use the information in the data table to finish the picture graph.

Cakes Baked Today

F Flavor of Cake	N Number of Cakes Baked
Chocolate	12
Vanilla	10
Lemon	6
Spice	2

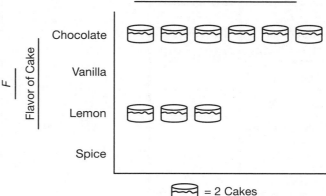

Cakes Baked Today

= 2 Cakes

2. What scale did Linda use to make her picture graph? _____

3. **A.** How many cake symbols did you have to draw on the graph to show 10 vanilla cakes?

   _____

   B. Show or tell how you know.

4. Write a number sentence to show the difference between the number of chocolate cakes Linda's mom baked and the number of spice cakes she baked.

_____

Check-In: Questions 5–10

5. The students in third grade were selling popcorn to raise money. They started to draw a data table and a picture graph to show how many bags of popcorn they sold each day. Use the information below to complete the missing parts of the data table and picture graph.

Popcorn Sales

D Day of the Week	N Number of Bags Sold
Monday	10
Tuesday	20
Wednesday	
Thursday	5
Friday	

Popcorn Sales

🍿 = 5 Bags of Popcorn

Use your graph and data table to answer the following questions.

6. A. How many popcorn bag symbols did you need to draw on the graph to show the number of bags sold on Tuesday? _____

B. Show or tell how you know.

7. A. How many bags of popcorn did the students sell on Friday? _____

B. Show or tell how you know.

8. A. How many bags of popcorn did the students sell on Monday and Tuesday?

_____

B. How does the total for Monday and Tuesday compare to the amount sold on Friday?

_____

C. Show or tell your thinking.

9. A. Write a number sentence to show how many bags of popcorn the students sold during all five days.

_____

B. Show or tell how to use your graph to answer Question 9A.

10. The students decide to sell popcorn during a second week.

    A. Predict the day of the week that will have the most sales.

    _____

    B. Show or tell how you know.

Picture Graphs Check-In: Questions 5–10 Feedback Box	Expectation	Check In	Comments
Draw scaled picture graphs from a table. [Q# 5]	E2		
Read a table or scaled graph to find information about a data set. [Q# 5–6]	E3		
Make predictions and generalizations about a population from a sample using data tables and graphs. [Q# 10]	E4		
Solve one- and two-step problems using data in scaled picture graphs. [Q# 7–9]	E5		

Unit 2
Strategies

	Practice	
	Daily Practice and Problems	**Home Practice**
Lesson 1: Addition Strategies	A–D	
Lesson 2: Strategies for Making Tens	E–H	
Lesson 3: Spinning Sums	I–L	Parts 1–2
Lesson 4: Magic Squares	M–P	
Lesson 5: Subtraction Facts Strategies	Q–T	Parts 3–4
Lesson 6: Spinning Differences	U–X	
Lesson 7: Workshop: Reasoning from Known Facts	Y–Z	
Lesson 8: Assessing the Subtracting Facts	AA–BB	

Math Facts

Practice the subtraction facts in Group 1 ($12 - 9$, $12 - 10$, $13 - 9$, $13 - 10$, $13 - 4$, $15 - 9$, $15 - 10$, $15 - 6$, $19 - 10$) and Group 2 ($14 - 10$, $14 - 9$, $14 - 5$, $17 - 10$, $17 - 9$, $11 - 9$, $16 - 9$, $16 - 7$, $16 - 10$).

Name _____

Date _____

Number Lines 0 – 30

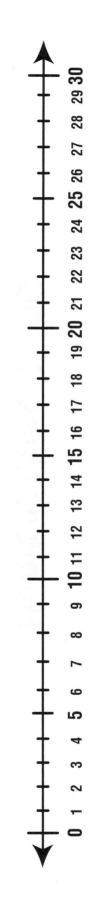

Number Lines 0 – 30

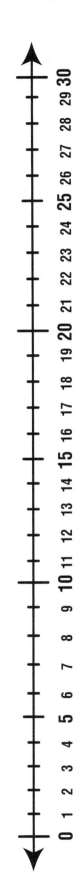

Using Addition Strategies

1. Find the missing numbers. You may use the *Number Lines 0–30* page to help you solve the problems.

A. ☐ = 10 + 2

B. 22 = ☐ + 2

C. 8 + 4 = 8 + ☐ + 2

D. 8 + 4 = ☐ + 2

E. 6 + ☐ = 8 + 7

F. 18 + 4 = 20 + ☐

2. Show or tell how you solved Question 1F.

3. Draw a circle around the numbers that make tens in the first problem in each pair. Then complete both number sentences. The first one is an example.

Ex. (6 + 4) + 2 = ☐   10 + ☐2☐ = 12

A. 4 + 7 + 3 = ☐   4 + ☐ = 14

B. 5 + 11 + 9 = ☐   ☐ + 20 = 25

C. 18 + 2 + 6 = ☐   ☐ + 6 = 26

D. 25 + 5 + 2 = ☐   30 + ☐ = 32

E. 5 + 21 + 9 = ☐   5 + ☐ = 35

Switch It!

1. Complete the following problems in your head. Try to use a ten whenever possible.

   A. 3 + 16 + 7 = _____

   B. 9 + 17 + 1 = _____

   C. 2 + 11 + 8 = _____

   D. 5 + 15 + 6 = _____

   E. 7 + 12 + 8 = _____

2. Choose two problems from above and tell how you solved each one. You can use pictures, words, or number sentences and the space below the problem to explain.

3. Write and solve your own addition problem.

Section III

Name _____ Date _____

Six Key Is Broken

Imagine the six key on your calculator is broken. What keystrokes would you press to do the problems below? Look for tens.
For example, 7 + 16 + 4 could be solved by pressing:

| 7 | + | 3 | + | 13 | + | 4 | = |

List your keystrokes and write the sum. You do not have to fill all the boxes.

1. 6 + 15 + 2 = _____

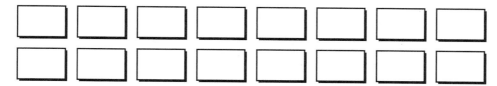

2. 17 + 6 + 4 = _____

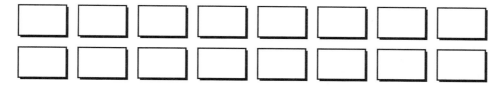

3. 14 + 6 + 7 = _____

4. 6 + 18 + 1 = _____

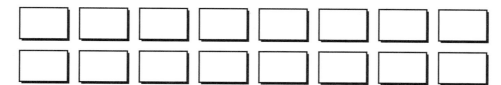

Spinning Sums Lab

Work with your group to look for patterns in sums when you spin matching spinners.

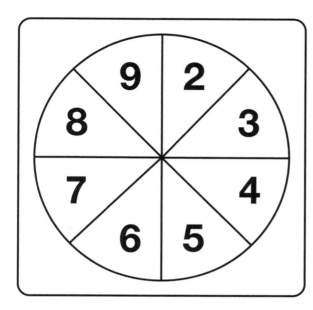 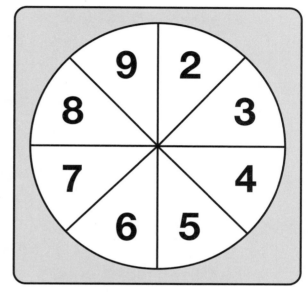

Discuss

1. Which spinner will you use for the first number in your number sentence?

   _____

2. How many times will you spin each spinner? _____

> Remember to keep track of your spins.

Name _____

Date _____

Collect

Tally My Spins

Sum	Number Sentence	How Many?

Name

Date

Graph

Name

Date

Graph

More Magic Squares

1. Use what you have learned about magic squares and the digits 4, 6, 8, and 9 to complete this magic square.

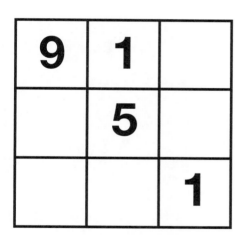

7	12	5
		10
11		

2. Here is another incomplete magic square.

A. Fill in the empty boxes to make a magic square that has three 1s, three 5s, and three 9s.

B. Find another solution for the blank magic square below that also uses the digits 1, 1, 1, 5, 5, 5, 9, 9, 9.

C. Show or tell the strategy you used to find the sum of each row, column, and diagonal.

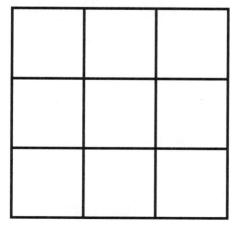

9	1	
	5	
		1

3. A. Fill in the empty boxes.
This magic square uses the digits
3, 3, 3, 7, 7, 7, 11, 11, 11.

B. Show or tell the patterns you used to
help you complete the square.

3	11	7
		11

4. Arrange 1, 2, 3, 4, 5, 6, 7, 8, 9 into a magic square that is different from
the one on the back of the turtle.

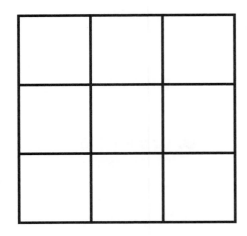

5. Challenge:

A. Find as many different magic squares as you can with the numbers
from the square in Question 2.

B. Find as many different magic squares as you can with the numbers
from the square in Question 3.

C. How are the solutions to the magic squares in Parts A and B alike?

Homework

Dear Family Member:
Magic squares are ancient number puzzles that have intrigued
people for thousands of years. In a magic square, the numbers
in the rows, columns, and diagonals all have the same sum.
Here is a magic square with the sum 15. Thank you.

2	7	6
9	5	1
4	3	8

1. Here is an incomplete magic square:

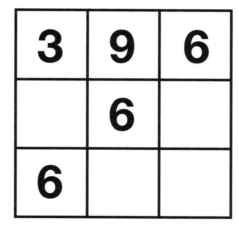

A. What is the sum of the first row? _____

B. Use 3, 3, 9, and 9 to complete the magic square. Remember that
each row, column, and diagonal must have the same sum.

2. Which of the following is a magic square?

A.

7	14	9
12	10	8
11	6	13

B.

11	6	13
7	11	15
14	10	9

Explain why the other puzzle is not a magic square.

3. Here is an incomplete magic square.

    A. What is its sum? _____

    B. Use the digits 5, 7, 11, and 12 to complete the magic square.

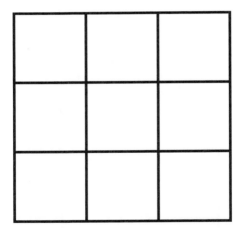

4. Find a different magic square that uses the same sum and numbers as the one in Question 3. Use the digits 5, 6, 7, 8, 9, 10, 11, 12, 13.

Nine, Ten Game

This is a game for two players. The object of the game is to be the first person to fill in one of the columns on his or her game board.

Materials

- Spinners 11–18 and 9–10 below
- 2 clear plastic spinners or 2 pencils with paper clips
- *Nine, Ten Game Boards* for each player

First Spin

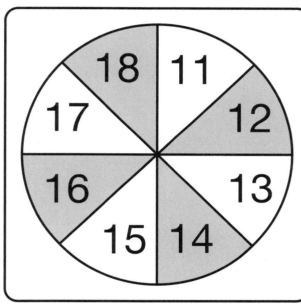

Second Spin

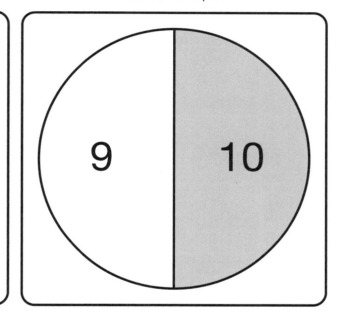

Directions

1. Player 1 spins both spinners. On the first spinner, you will spin a number from 11 to 18. On the second spinner, you will spin either a 9 or a 10.

2. Say a subtraction sentence with the two numbers you spin.

3. If your partner agrees that your answer is correct, write the number sentence in the game board column where it belongs. If your answer is not correct, do not write anything on the game board.

4. Players take turns repeating steps 1–3. The first player to fill in one of the columns on his or her game board is the winner.

Nine, Ten Game Boards

Subtract 9	Subtract 10

Subtract 9	Subtract 10

Subtract 9	Subtract 10

Subtract 9	Subtract 10

Nine, Ten Game Boards

Subtract 9	Subtract 10

Subtract 9	Subtract 10

Subtract 9	Subtract 10

Subtract 9	Subtract 10

Name _____ Date _____

Related Facts

 Homework

Dear Family Member:
The set of math facts you can make from the same numbers is called a *fact family*.
Here is the fact family for the numbers 2, 7, and 9:

$$2 + 7 = 9 \qquad 7 + 2 = 9$$
$$9 - 7 = 2 \qquad 9 - 2 = 7$$

Thinking of related facts together helps students remember them. Thank you.

1. Complete the following sentences to make fact families. Make four
different sentences in each group:

A. $7 + 4 = \boxed{}$

$4 + \boxed{} = 11$

$\boxed{} - 4 = 7$

$11 - 7 = \boxed{}$

B. $3 + 6 = \boxed{}$

$6 + \boxed{} = 9$

$\boxed{} - 6 = 3$

$\boxed{} - 3 = 6$

C. $\boxed{} + 8 = 14$

$8 + 6 = \boxed{}$

$14 - 6 = \boxed{}$

$\boxed{} - 8 = \boxed{}$

2. Write the four number sentences in the fact families for the following numbers:

A. 4, 5, 9

_____   _____

_____   _____

B. 2, 8, 10

_____   _____

_____   _____

C. 6, 7, 13

_____   _____

_____   _____

Spinning Differences Lab

Work with your partner to look for patterns in the differences when you spin matching spinners.

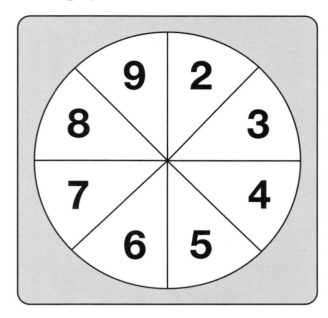
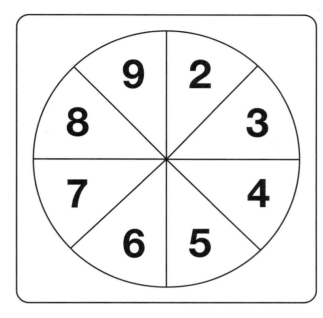

1. Make a prediction: what will be the most common difference?

_____

2. Make a prediction: what will be the least common difference?

_____

 **Draw**

Draw a picture of the lab setup.

- How many times will you spin the spinner?
- How will you show your data?

Name _____

Date _____

Labels?
Title?

Explore

3. Which difference occurred most often? _____

4. Which difference occurred least often? _____

5. Show or tell how you used tools and strategies to answer Questions 3 and 4. Write your explanation on the back of your graph.

6. Complete a chart that shows all the different subtraction number sentences you could get for each difference using the spinners below.

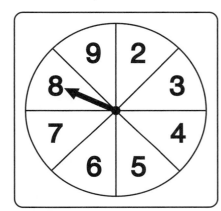
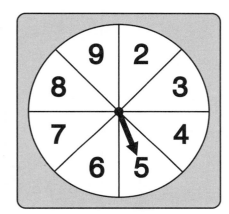

9 – 9							
9 – 8							
	9 – 7						
		9 – 6					
			9 – 5				
5 – 4				9 – 4			
3 – 3	4 – 3				9 – 3		
2 – 2	3 – 2	4 – 2	5 – 2	6 – 2	7 – 2	8 – 2	9 – 2
0	**1**	**2**	**3**	**4**	**5**	**6**	**7**

7. Which difference on the chart has the most number sentences? _____

8. Which difference has the fewest number sentences? _____

9. Look at the number sentences that have zero as the difference. Describe these number sentences. Write your description on the back of your graph.

Name _____ Date _____

Spinning Differences Lab
Feedback Box

	Expectation	Check In	Comments
Make predictions and generalizations using tables and graphs. [Questions 1–4, Data Table, and Graph]	E1		
Identify patterns in differences. [Data Table]	E3		

	Yes . . .	Yes, but . . .	No, but . . .	No . . .
MPE2. Find a strategy. I choose good tools and an efficient strategy for solving the problem. [Question 5]				
MPE5. Show my work. I show or tell how I arrived at my answer so someone else can understand my thinking. [Question 5]				

What Is the Difference?

Homework

Carla and Nisha used two different spinners to make subtraction number sentences. Write a subtraction number sentence for each of their spins.

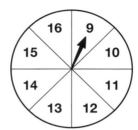 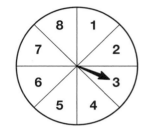   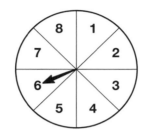 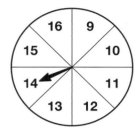

1. _____   **2.** _____

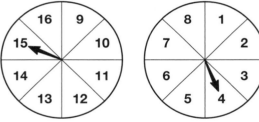   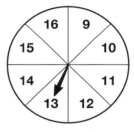 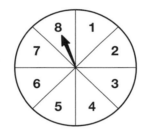

3. _____   **4.** _____

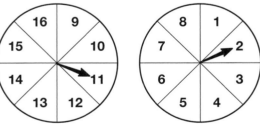    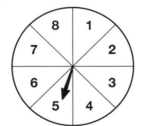

5. _____   **6.** _____

7. Look at the numbers on the spinners in Question 6. Will you ever be able to spin a number sentence that will have a difference of zero? Show or tell how you know.

Spinning Differences   **SAB • Grade 3 • Unit 2 • Lesson 6**   **61**

Reasoning from Known Facts
Workshop Menu

- Look at each row in the table.
- For each row, decide whether you are "Working On It," you are "Getting It," or you already "Got It."
- Remember, you may feel you are "Working On It" for one row, but for another row, you already "Got It."
- On this table, draw a circle around each set of problems you decide to do.
- If one set of problems seems too easy or too hard, choose a different set from the same row.

Workshop Menu			
Can I Do This?	**▲ Working On It!** I could use some extra help. *Romesh*	**● Getting It!** I just need some more practice. *Linda*	**■ Got It!** I'm ready for a challenge. *Jacob*
Use tens to subtract.	**Questions 1–6, 11–14**	**Questions 3–6, 11–16**	**Questions 12, 14–17**
Think addition to subtract.	**Questions 7–10, 18**	**Questions 7–10, 18–19**	**Questions 7–9, 18–21**

Using Subtraction Strategies

Using Tens

▲☐☐ **1.** **A.** Solve each problem below. Write a number sentence that shows your solution.

Number	Subtract 10 Number sentence	Subtract 9 Number sentence	Subtract 8 Number sentence
16	16 – 10 = 6	16 – 10 + 1 = 7	16 – 10 + 2 = 8
13			
17			
15			

B. Describe a pattern you see for subtracting 10.

C. Look at the answers for subtracting 9. How are they different from the answers for subtracting 10?

D. Look at the answers for subtracting 8. How are they different from the answers for subtracting 10?

E. Describe the pattern you see in the number sentences in each column.

▲☐☐ **2.** Show or tell how you use ten to solve 13 − 9.

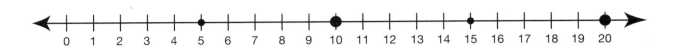

▲●☐ **3.** Luis started to show how he used ten and the number line to solve 13 − 8. Use the number line and boxes to help Luis complete his strategy below.

For 13 − 8, I use ten.

13 − 10 = 3

I took away too much. I took away 2 more than I should have.

I have to put 2 back.

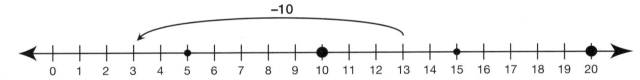

Two small hops forward and I land on ☐ .

13 − 8 = ☐

▲●☐ **4.** John solved 17 − 9 this way.

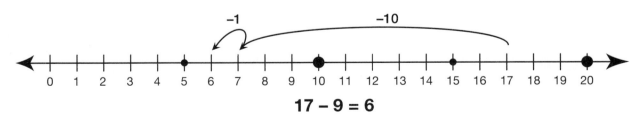

17 − 9 = 6

Do you agree with John? _____

If not, show or tell how you would help John.

△●□ 5. Frank solved 14 − 8 this way:

"I thought about addition. I know 8 + 6 = 14. So 14 − 8 = 6."

Do you agree with Frank? _____

If not, show or tell how you would help Frank.

△●□ 6. Show how you can solve 15 − 7.

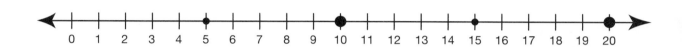

Thinking Addition

 ## Check-In: Questions 7–9

△●■ 7. Natasha solved 24 − 9 this way on the *200 Chart*.

1	2	3	4	5	6	7	8	9	10
11	12	13	14	15	16	17	18	19	20
21	22	23	24	25	26	27	28	29	30
	32	33	34	35	36		38	39	40

24 − 10 = 14
14 − 1 = 13
24 − 9 = 13

Do you agree with Natasha? _____

If not, show or tell how you would help Natasha.

▲|●|■ **8.** Solve 24 − 9 another way.

▲|●|■ **9.** Yolanda solved 12 − 7 this way. Help Yolanda complete her strategy.

She started at 7 and counted up on the number line.

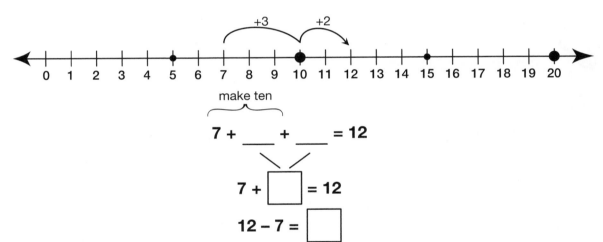

7 + ___ **+** ___ **= 12**

7 + [ ] **= 12**

12 − 7 = [ ]

▲|●| **10.** Show how you solve 13 − 5.

Using Tens with Larger Numbers

▲●☐ 11. A. Solve each problem in the table. Write a number sentence that shows your strategies.

	Subtract 10	Subtract 9
Number	**Number sentence**	**Number sentence**
22	22 − 10 = 12	22 − 10 + 1 = 13
25		
33		
37		

B. Describe the pattern you see for subtracting 10.

C. How are the answers for subtracting 9 different from the answers for subtracting 10?

▲●■ 12. Solve each problem in the table. Write a number sentence that shows your strategy.

	Subtract 20	Subtract 19
Number	**Number sentence**	**Number sentence**
22	22 − 20 = 2	22 − 20 + 1 = 3
25		
33		
37		

Name _____ Date _____

▲● 13. Michael had a collection of 16 marbles. He lost 9 marbles. How many marbles did he have left? Michael started to solve the problem below. Help him complete his strategy. Show Michael's solution strategy on the number line.

Taking away 10 is one more than I need to take away.

Michael

$16 - 10 = 6$

$16 - 10 + \boxed{} = 7$

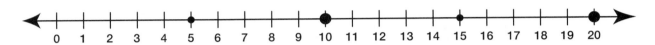

✔ Check-In: Question 14

▲●■ 14. Show how you can solve 33 − 13 on the number line.

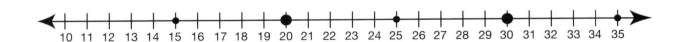

●■ 15. Show how you can solve 33 − 14 on the number line.

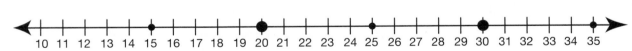

●■ 16. Richard solved 33 − 14 this way. "I know that 33 − 13 = 20, so 33 − 14 = 21."

Do you agree with Richard? _____

If not, show or tell how you can help Richard.

■ **17.** Show how you can solve 30 – 19 on the number line.

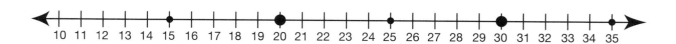

Thinking Addition with Larger Numbers

 Check-In: Question 18

▲●■ **18.** Carla started to show how she solved 30 – 17. Help Carla complete her strategy below on the number line. She started at 17 and counted up.

make twenty

$17 + \underline{} + \underline{} = 30$

$17 + \boxed{} = 30$

$30 - 17 = \boxed{}$

■● ■ **19.** Show or tell how you solve 42 – 16.

20. Show or tell how you solve 26 – 13.

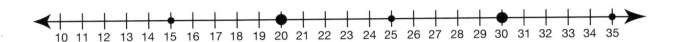

21. Fern started to solve 51 – 12 on the number line below. Help Fern complete her strategy on the number line.

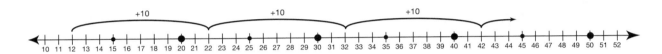

Can you show or tell a different strategy for 51 – 12?

Name _____ Date _____

Kim's and Suzanne's Marbles

Homework

Choose one group of problems to complete.

Workshop Menu		
Can I Do This?	**▲ Working On It!** I could use some extra help. *Carla*	**● Getting It!** I just need some more practice. *Natasha*
Use facts I know to solve problems.	**Questions 4–7**	**Questions 1–3**

Solve each problem using the number line. Write a number sentence that shows your solution strategy.

Suzanne has a jar of 27 marbles. Start each problem with 27 marbles.

1. If Suzanne takes 10 marbles out of the jar, how many are left in the jar?

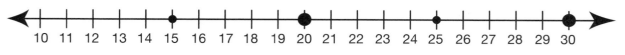

Number sentence: _____

2. If she takes 8 marbles out of the jar, how many are left in the jar?

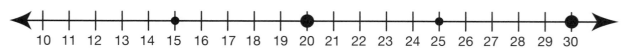

Number sentence: _____

3. If she takes 11 marbles out of the jar, how many are left in the jar?

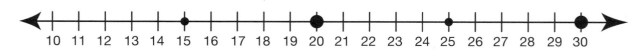

Number sentence: _____

Name _____ Date _____

Solve each problem using the number line. Write a number sentence that shows your solution strategy.

Kim has a jar of 17 marbles. Start each problem with 17 marbles.

[△]▢▢ **4.** If Kim takes 10 marbles out of the jar, how many are left in the jar?

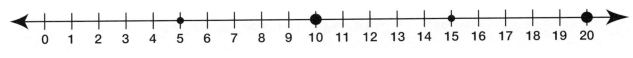

Number sentence: _____

[△]▢▢ **5.** If she takes 9 marbles out of the jar, how many are left in the jar?

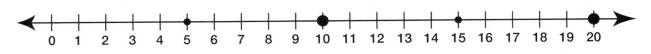

Number sentence: _____

[△]▢▢ **6.** If she takes 8 marbles out of the jar, how many are left in the jar?

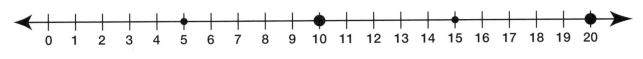

Number sentence: _____

[△]▢▢ **7.** If she takes 11 marbles out of the jar, how many are left in the jar?

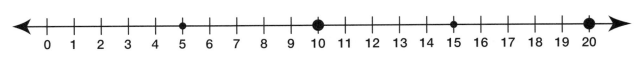

Number sentence: _____

Name _____

Date _____

Sorting Flash Cards Board

Facts I Know Quickly	Facts I Can Figure Out	Facts I Need to Learn

Subtraction Facts I Know

Circle the subtraction facts you know and can answer quickly. Underline the facts you can figure out using a strategy. Do nothing to the facts you still need to learn.

	A	B	C	D	E	F	G	H
2	$\begin{array}{r}4\\-2\\\hline 2\end{array}$	$\begin{array}{r}5\\-2\\\hline 3\end{array}$	$\begin{array}{r}6\\-2\\\hline 4\end{array}$	$\begin{array}{r}7\\-2\\\hline 5\end{array}$	$\begin{array}{r}8\\-2\\\hline 6\end{array}$	$\begin{array}{r}9\\-2\\\hline 7\end{array}$	$\begin{array}{r}10\\-2\\\hline 8\end{array}$	$\begin{array}{r}11\\-2\\\hline 9\end{array}$
3	$\begin{array}{r}5\\-3\\\hline 2\end{array}$	$\begin{array}{r}6\\-3\\\hline 3\end{array}$	$\begin{array}{r}7\\-3\\\hline 4\end{array}$	$\begin{array}{r}8\\-3\\\hline 5\end{array}$	$\begin{array}{r}9\\-3\\\hline 6\end{array}$	$\begin{array}{r}10\\-3\\\hline 7\end{array}$	$\begin{array}{r}11\\-3\\\hline 8\end{array}$	$\begin{array}{r}12\\-3\\\hline 9\end{array}$
4	$\begin{array}{r}6\\-4\\\hline 2\end{array}$	$\begin{array}{r}7\\-4\\\hline 3\end{array}$	$\begin{array}{r}8\\-4\\\hline 4\end{array}$	$\begin{array}{r}9\\-4\\\hline 5\end{array}$	$\begin{array}{r}10\\-4\\\hline 6\end{array}$	$\begin{array}{r}11\\-4\\\hline 7\end{array}$	$\begin{array}{r}12\\-4\\\hline 8\end{array}$	$\begin{array}{r}13\\-4\\\hline 9\end{array}$
5	$\begin{array}{r}7\\-5\\\hline 2\end{array}$	$\begin{array}{r}8\\-5\\\hline 3\end{array}$	$\begin{array}{r}9\\-5\\\hline 4\end{array}$	$\begin{array}{r}10\\-5\\\hline 5\end{array}$	$\begin{array}{r}11\\-5\\\hline 6\end{array}$	$\begin{array}{r}12\\-5\\\hline 7\end{array}$	$\begin{array}{r}13\\-5\\\hline 8\end{array}$	$\begin{array}{r}14\\-5\\\hline 9\end{array}$
6	$\begin{array}{r}8\\-6\\\hline 2\end{array}$	$\begin{array}{r}9\\-6\\\hline 3\end{array}$	$\begin{array}{r}10\\-6\\\hline 4\end{array}$	$\begin{array}{r}11\\-6\\\hline 5\end{array}$	$\begin{array}{r}12\\-6\\\hline 6\end{array}$	$\begin{array}{r}13\\-6\\\hline 7\end{array}$	$\begin{array}{r}14\\-6\\\hline 8\end{array}$	$\begin{array}{r}15\\-6\\\hline 9\end{array}$
7	$\begin{array}{r}9\\-7\\\hline 2\end{array}$	$\begin{array}{r}10\\-7\\\hline 3\end{array}$	$\begin{array}{r}11\\-7\\\hline 4\end{array}$	$\begin{array}{r}12\\-7\\\hline 5\end{array}$	$\begin{array}{r}13\\-7\\\hline 6\end{array}$	$\begin{array}{r}14\\-7\\\hline 7\end{array}$	$\begin{array}{r}15\\-7\\\hline 8\end{array}$	$\begin{array}{r}16\\-7\\\hline 9\end{array}$
8	$\begin{array}{r}10\\-8\\\hline 2\end{array}$	$\begin{array}{r}11\\-8\\\hline 3\end{array}$	$\begin{array}{r}12\\-8\\\hline 4\end{array}$	$\begin{array}{r}13\\-8\\\hline 5\end{array}$	$\begin{array}{r}14\\-8\\\hline 6\end{array}$	$\begin{array}{r}15\\-8\\\hline 7\end{array}$	$\begin{array}{r}16\\-8\\\hline 8\end{array}$	$\begin{array}{r}17\\-8\\\hline 9\end{array}$
9	$\begin{array}{r}11\\-9\\\hline 2\end{array}$	$\begin{array}{r}12\\-9\\\hline 3\end{array}$	$\begin{array}{r}13\\-9\\\hline 4\end{array}$	$\begin{array}{r}14\\-9\\\hline 5\end{array}$	$\begin{array}{r}15\\-9\\\hline 6\end{array}$	$\begin{array}{r}16\\-9\\\hline 7\end{array}$	$\begin{array}{r}17\\-9\\\hline 8\end{array}$	$\begin{array}{r}18\\-9\\\hline 9\end{array}$
10	$\begin{array}{r}12\\-10\\\hline 2\end{array}$	$\begin{array}{r}13\\-10\\\hline 3\end{array}$	$\begin{array}{r}14\\-10\\\hline 4\end{array}$	$\begin{array}{r}15\\-10\\\hline 5\end{array}$	$\begin{array}{r}16\\-10\\\hline 6\end{array}$	$\begin{array}{r}17\\-10\\\hline 7\end{array}$	$\begin{array}{r}18\\-10\\\hline 8\end{array}$	$\begin{array}{r}19\\-10\\\hline 9\end{array}$

Name _____ Date _____

Fact Families

A fact family is a set of four related number sentences. For example, the following four sentences form a fact family:

$$3 + 4 = 7, 4 + 3 = 7, 7 - 4 = 3, \text{ and } 7 - 3 = 4.$$

Complete the number sentences for the fact families.

1. **A.** $9 +$ _____ $= 15$ **B.** _____ $+$ _____ $= 15$

    C. $15 -$ _____ $=$ _____   **D.** $15 -$ _____ $=$ _____

2. **A.** $13 -$ _____ $= 4$ **B.** $13 -$ _____ $=$ _____

    C. _____ $+$ _____ $= 13$ **D.** _____ $+$ _____ $= 13$

3. Explain the strategy or strategies you used to solve Question 2A.

4. Choose a subtraction fact and write the four related addition and subtraction number sentences.

    A. _____   **B.** _____

    C. _____   **D.** _____

Unit 3

Exploring Multiplication

	Practice	
	Daily Practice and Problems	**Home Practice**
Lesson 1: T-Shirt Factory Problems	A–B	
Lesson 2: In Twos, Threes, and More	C–H	Parts 1–2
Lesson 3: Multiplication Stories	I–L	
Lesson 4: Making Teams	M–N	Part 3
Lesson 5: Multiples on the Calendar	O–P	Part 4
Lesson 6: Workshop: Multiplication and Division Stories	Q–R	

Math Facts

Practice the subtraction facts in Group 3 (10 – 4, 9 – 4, 11– 4, 10 – 8, 11 – 8, 9 – 5, 10 – 6, 11 – 6, 11 – 5) and Group 4 (10 – 7, 9 – 7, 11 – 7, 10 – 2, 9 – 2, 9 – 3, 10 – 3, 11 – 3, 9 – 6).

Develop number sense strategies for the multiplication facts for the 5s and 10s.

Family T-Shirts

Homework

Dear Family Member:

In class, we solved problems using the number of letters in our first names. Please help your child spell each family member's name on the T-shirts he or she draws for the family. Your child will use these drawings, repeated addition, and other mental math strategies to solve Questions 2 and 3.

Thank you.

1. Imagine your family is making T-shirts with their names on them. Draw pictures of all the T-shirts your family will need. Use the back of this page or other paper for your pictures.

2. If each letter costs 10¢, how much will the letters for your shirt cost? Explain your solution.

3. How much will the letters for all of your family cost? Explain how you got your answer.

In Twos Through Twelves

 Homework

Dear Family Member:

We are working with things that come in groups. For example, wheels on a bicycle come in groups of two. Have your child look for things around your house that come in groups. Then have your child fill in as much of the table as he or she can. You can help by suggesting other items that come in groups.

Thank you.

List things that come in:

Groups of	Examples
Two	
Three	
Four	
Five	

Groups of	Examples
Six	
Seven	
Eight	
Nine	
Ten	
Eleven	
Twelve	

Using Multiplication to Count Things in Groups

1. A spider has 8 legs. How many legs are there on 5 spiders altogether? Draw the spiders and write a number sentence to show your thinking.

Number Sentence _____

2. Think of something that comes in groups of a number other than 8. You can use something from your list *In Twos Through Twelves* or think of something different.

A. Draw several groups of the thing you have chosen.

B. Write a multiplication story that matches your picture.

C. Write a multiplication sentence to show your thinking.

_____

3. Fill in the boxes to make the following sentences true:

A. 10 + 10 + 10 + 10 = ☐ × 10   **B.** 6 + 6 + 6 + 6 + 6 = 5 × ☐

C. ☐ + 8 = 2 × 8   **D.** 7 + 7 + 7 = ☐ × 7

Number Sentences

Complete the following addition and multiplication sentences. Make sure that they are true sentences when you are done.

A. 2 + 2 + 2 + 2 = ☐ × 2

B. 2 × 5 = ☐ + 5

C. 6 + 6 + 6 = ☐ × 6

D. 7 + 7 + 7 + 7 = ☐ × 7

E. 3 × ☐ = 1 + 1 + 1

F. 1 × 8 = ☐

G. 10 = ☐ × 10

H. 2 × 9 = ☐ + 9

I. 4 + 4 + 4 + 4 + 4 = ☐ × 4

J. 3 + 3 + 3 = 3 × ☐

K. Think of things that come in groups of three. Solve the problem below and write a story for the number sentence.

3 + 3 + 3 + 3 + 3 =

Class Teams Table

Record your class size and complete the data table.

Class Size _____

Number of Teams	Team Size	Remainder	Number Sentence
	2		
	3		
	4		
	5		

Look at your table. Circle any factors of the number you used as your class size.

Name _____   Date _____

Multiplication and Division Stories Workshop Menu

Use the questions in the table below to check your progress with solving multiplication and division problems.

- For each row decide whether you are "Working On It" or you are "Getting It."
- Remember, you may feel you are "Working On It" for one row, but for another row, you are "Getting It."
- Use an "X" to show your decision.

Workshop Menu		
Can I Do This?	▲ **Working On It!** I could use some extra help. *Peter*	● **Getting It!** I just need some more practice. *Natasha*
Use drawings to show stories.		
Use number sentences to show stories.		
Solve problems.		
Show solution strategies with drawings and number sentences.		

Copyright © Kendall Hunt Publishing Company

Unit 4

Place Value Concepts

Lesson		Practice	
		Daily Practice and Problems	Home Practice
Lesson 1: Tens and Ones		A–B	Parts 1–2
Lesson 2: Hundreds, Tens, and Ones		C–F	
Lesson 3: Thousands, Hundreds, Tens, and Ones		G–H	
Lesson 4: Comparing and Writing Numbers		I–J	
Lesson 5: Base-Ten Hoppers		K–N	
Lesson 6: Workshop: Place Value		O–T	
Lesson 7: Number Sense With Dollars and Cents		U–V	Parts 3–4

Math Facts

Use the practice in this unit to review the subtraction facts for Group 5 ($7 - 3$, $7 - 5$, $7 - 2$, $11 - 2$, $8 - 6$, $5 - 3$, $8 - 2$, $4 - 2$, $5 - 2$) and Group 6 ($6 - 4$, $6 - 2$, $13 - 5$, $8 - 5$, $8 - 3$, $13 - 8$, $12 - 8$, $12 - 4$, $12 - 3$) and to develop number sense strategies for the multiplication facts for the 2s and 3s.

Packaging Sheets

Number = _26_

🝙🝙🝙🝙🝙🝙	🝙
	26
1	16
2	6

Number = ____

🝙🝙🝙🝙🝙🝙	🝙

Number = ____

🝙🝙🝙🝙🝙🝙	🝙

Number = ____

🝙🝙🝙🝙🝙🝙	🝙

Number = ____

🝙🝙🝙🝙🝙🝙	🝙

Number = ____

🝙🝙🝙🝙🝙🝙	🝙

Number = ____

🝙🝙🝙🝙🝙🝙	🝙

Number = ____

🝙🝙🝙🝙🝙🝙	🝙

Number = ____

🝙🝙🝙🝙🝙🝙	🝙

Pack 'Em Up!

Help Eric package the Chocos he made at the **TIMS Candy Company. In each problem, circle the bits Eric can package together to make skinnies. Draw the skinnies and cross out the bits. Then record the skinnies and bits on Eric's Packaging Sheets. The first one is an example.**

Ex.

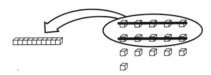

Eric's Packaging Sheet

	16
1	6

1.

Eric's Packaging Sheet

2.

Eric's Packaging Sheet

3.

Eric's Packaging Sheet

Professor Peabody was helping package Chocos at the TIMS Candy Company. He wrote the different ways he could package the Chocos on the packaging sheets. Some of the numbers were written with invisible ink. Help fill in the missing numbers. The first one is an example.

Ex.

▭	▢
	32
1	22
2	12
3	2

4.

▭	▢
	24
	14
2	

5.

▭	▢
1	37
	27
	17
4	

6.

▭	▢
	29
1	9

7. Maruta made 43 Chocos. She wrote down all the different ways 43 Chocos can be packaged. Then, she showed the first two partitions using number sentences. Write number sentences for the other partitions.

▭	▢
	43
1	33
2	23
3	13
4	3

$43 = 10 + 33$

$43 = 20 + 23$

_____

_____

8. Show all the different ways you can package 27 Chocos on the following packaging sheet. Write number sentences showing the partitions.

27

_____

_____

_____

✓ Check-In: Question 9

9. Show all the different ways you can package 45 Chocos on the following packaging sheet. Write number sentences showing the partitions.

45

_____

_____

_____

_____

10. For Questions 4–9, circle the partition in the table that uses the fewest packages. (For example, the partition of 32 into 1 skinny and 22 bits uses 23 packages.) Look for a pattern that describes the partition that uses the fewest packages. Be ready to talk about the pattern you found.

Make a Flat

The object of the game is to be the first player to fill the flat. This is a game for two players.

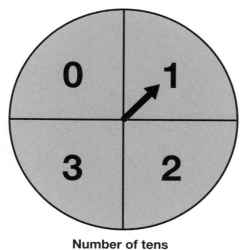

Number of tens

Number of ones

Materials

- 1 Make a Flat Game Board for each player
- 1 gray spinner with 0–3 for tens
- 1 white spinner with 0–9 for ones
- clear plastic spinner or pencil and paper clip
- 20 bits, 20 skinnies, and 1 flat

Directions

1. Spin the gray spinner once and take that many skinnies. Spin the white spinner once and take that many bits.

2. Line up your skinnies and bits on your game board.

3. Trade bits for skinnies according to the Fewest Pieces Rule.

4. After each turn, write the total number of base-ten pieces you have in the "Running Total" column.

5. Take turns repeating the steps above.

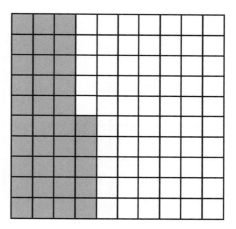

Turn	Running Total
1	23
2	35
3	
4	
5	
6	
7	

A sample game board after two spins

Make a Flat Game Board

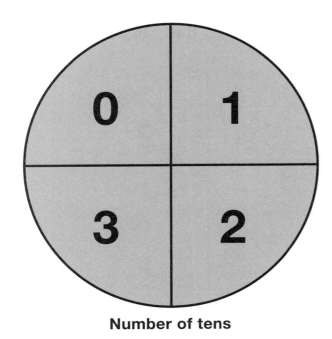

Number of tens

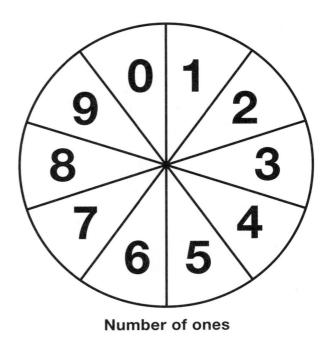

Number of ones

Turn	Running Total
1	
2	
3	
4	
5	
6	
7	
8	
9	
10	

Make a Pack

The object of the game is to be the first player to complete a pack. This is a game for two players.

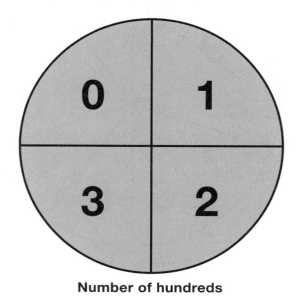

Number of hundreds

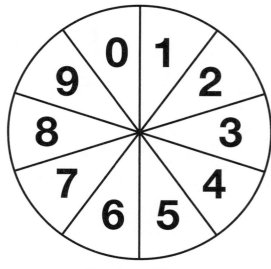

Number of tens

Materials

- 1 Make a Pack Game Board for each player
- 1 gray spinner with 0–3 for hundreds
- 1 white spinner with 0–9 for tens
- clear plastic spinner or pencil and paper clip
- 20 skinnies, 20 flats, and 1 pack

Directions

1. Spin the gray spinner once and take that many flats. Spin the white spinner once and take that many skinnies.

2. Stack up your flats and skinnies on your game board.

3. Trade skinnies for flats according to the Fewest Pieces Rule.

4. After each turn, write the total number of base-ten pieces you have in the "Running Total" column.

5. Take turns repeating the steps above.

Make a Pack Game Board

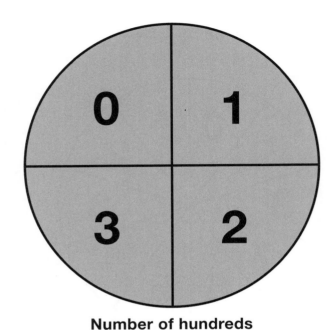

Number of hundreds

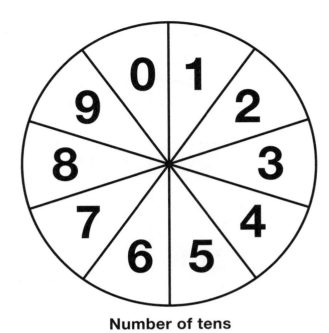

Number of tens

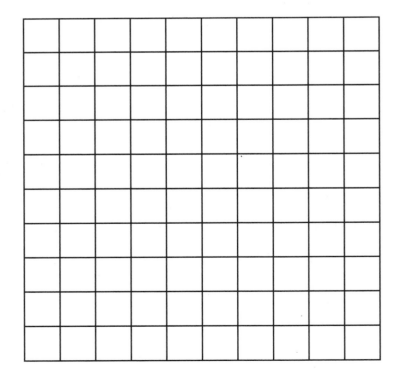

Turn	Running Total
1	
2	
3	
4	
5	
6	
7	
8	
9	
10	

Thousands, Hundreds, Tens, and Ones

Large Orders

1. Eric recorded his Choco orders on a Base-Ten Recording Sheet. The sheet below shows three ways he can package one of his orders. He wrote a number sentence to show the number of Chocos in the order. Complete his sheet with a number sentence for each of the other ways.

1000s	100s	10s	1s	Number Sentence
	2	3	7	$237 = 200 + 30 + 7$
	1	13	7	
	2	2	17	

2. For each Choco order below, write a number sentence to show the number ordered. Then write a different way to fill the order, along with a number sentence to match.

A.

1000s	100s	10s	1s	Number Sentence
2		5		

B.

1000s	100s	10s	1s	Number Sentence
3	4		7	

C.

1000s	100s	10s	1s	Number Sentence
6	2	5		

Base-ten piece	pack	flat	skinny	bit
Base-ten shorthand	▱	▯	│	•

3. Professor Peabody used base-ten shorthand to show the Chocos he made at the TIMS Candy Company. Figure out how many Chocos Professor Peabody made. Write a number sentence to show your answer.

A.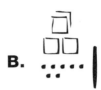

B.

4. Professor Peabody used base-ten shorthand to take an order for Chocos. Draw the same number of Chocos using the Fewest Pieces Rule. Then write down how many Chocos were made.

A. :::::: │

B.

C. ‖‖‖‖‖
‖‖‖‖‖
••

Name _____

Date _____

Spin, Place, and Read

The object of this game is to make the largest (or smallest) number with a set of digits.
This is a game for two to thirty players.

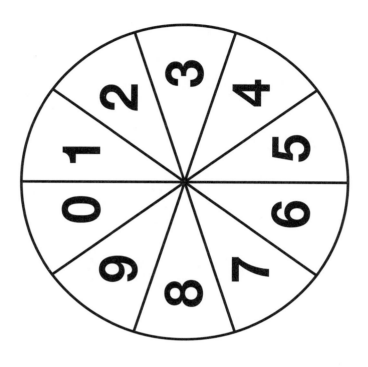

Materials

- clear plastic spinner or a pencil and paper clip
- Spin, Place, and Read Recording Sheet

Directions

- Choose one person to be the caller. For each round, the caller will spin the spinner one time for each box on the recording sheet.

- After each spin, record the digit in any one of the boxes. Once a digit is recorded, it cannot be moved.

- After the boxes in each round are filled, draw the number using base-ten shorthand. Read the number out loud.

- The player who makes the largest (or smallest) number wins. Circle the numbers in the rounds that you win.

Name _____

Date _____

Spin, Place, and Read Recording Sheet

Round		Base-Ten Shorthand
1. Largest		
2. Smallest		
3. Largest		
4. Largest		

Round	Base-Ten Shorthand		
5. Smallest			
6. Largest			
7. Largest			
8. Smallest			

Comparing and Writing Numbers

The Company Pays Its Bills

The TIMS Candy Company pays many bills. When writing a check, the amount is written in numbers and in words. Refer to the *Writing Numbers in Words* page in the *Student Guide* Reference section.

Here is a check for $502.00 to the Cocoa Supply Company.

TIMS Candy Company
555 E. Main Street
Chicago, IL 60600

109

June 8, 2015

PAY TO THE
ORDER OF _____ Cocoa Supply Company _____ $ 502.00

_____ Five hundred two _____ DOLLARS

Integrated Federal Bank

Memo _____

Tim Jones

Help the TIMS Candy Company by writing checks to the following companies.

1. Sugary Sweet Sugar Company for $487.00

TIMS Candy Company
555 E. Main Street
Chicago, IL 60600

110

_____

PAY TO THE
ORDER OF _____ $ ____

_____ DOLLARS

Integrated Federal Bank

Memo _____

2. Recycled Paper Company for $105.00

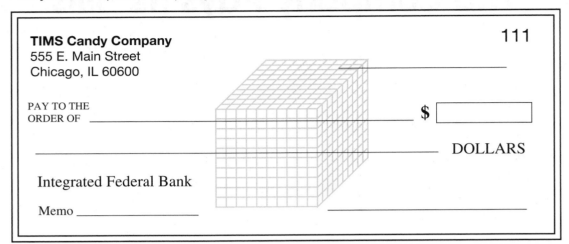

3. Box-It-Up Cardboard Company for $1006.00

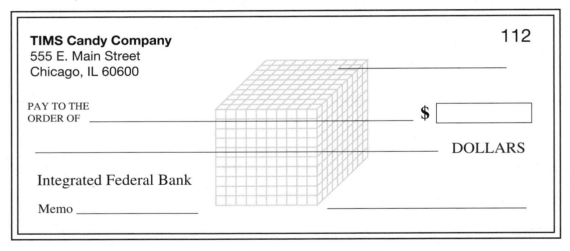

4. Bovine Dairy for $677.00

Helping Professor Peabody

Help Professor Peabody complete the number lines. Be sure that the distance and direction of each hop is clear. Then answer the questions.

1.

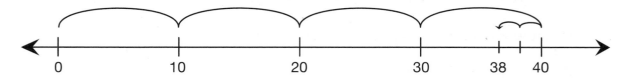

A. Show the distance and direction above each hop.

B. Draw a number line below that shows how a base-ten hopper can move from 0 to 38 another way.

2.

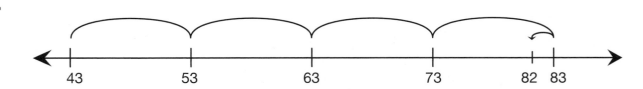

A. Show the distance and direction above each hop.

B. Show how a hopper can move from 43 to 82 another way.

C. How far is it from 43 to 82? _____

3.

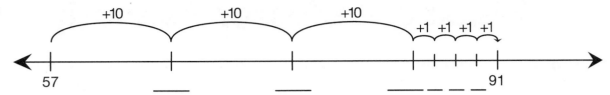

57 ____ ____ ____ ____ 91

A. Fill in the blanks to show where the base-ten hopper lands.

B. How far did the base-ten hopper move? _____

C. Complete the number sentence 57 + [ ] = 91.

D. Show another way for the base-ten hopper to move from 57 to 91.

4.

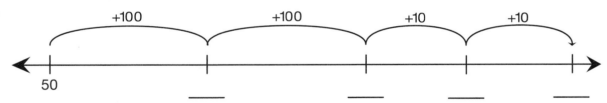

50 ____ ____ ____ ____

A. Fill in the blanks to show where the hopper lands.

B. How far is it from 50 to the point where the hopper stops?

_____

C. Show another way to start at 50 and go to the point where the hopper stops.

5.

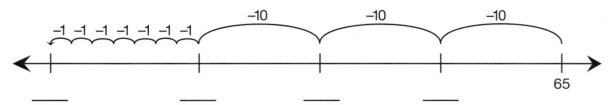

A. Fill in the blanks to show where the hopper lands.

B. How far is it from 65 to the point where the hopper stops?

_____

C. Show another way for a base-ten hopper to start at 65 and stop at the same point.

6.

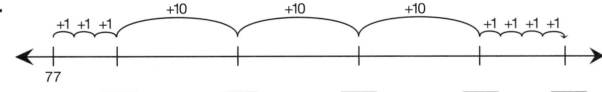

A. Fill in the blanks to show where the hopper lands.

B. How far is it from 77 to the point where the hopper stops?

_____

C. Show another way for a base-ten hopper to start at 77 and land at the same point.

![checkmark] **Check-In: Questions 7–10**

7. **A.** Show the distance and direction of each move above each hop on the number line.

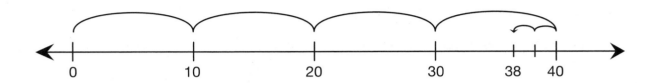

B. Write a number sentence that matches the moves on the number line.

Number Sentence: _____

C. Show how a base-ten hopper can move from 0 to 38 another way.

8. **A.** Show the distance and direction of each move above each hop on the number line below.

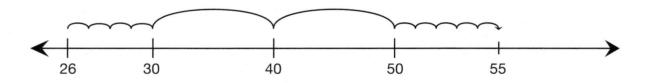

B. Show how a base-ten hopper can move from 26 to 55 another way.

C. How far is it from 26 to 55? _____

Name _____ Date _____

9. A. Fill in the blanks to show where the hopper lands on each hop on the number line below. (Hint: the hopper starts at 72.)

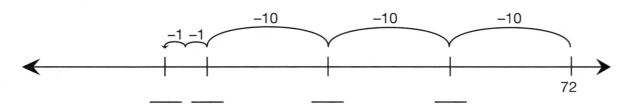

B. How far is it from 72 to where the hopper stops?

_____

C. Show another way for a base-ten hopper to start at 72 and stop at the same point.

10. A. Fill in the blanks to show where the hopper lands on each hop on the number line below.

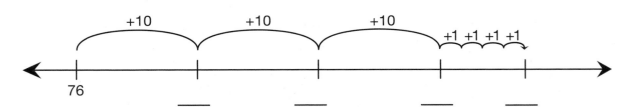

B. How far is it from 76 to where the hopper stops?

_____

C. Show another way for a base-ten hopper to start at 76 and stop at the same point.

Place Value
Workshop Menu

- Look at each row in the table.
- For each row, decide whether you are "Working On It," you are "Getting It," or you already "Got It."
- Remember, you may feel you are "Working On It" for one row, but for another row, you have already "Got It."
- On this table, draw a circle around each set of problems you decide to do.
- If one set of problems seems too easy or too hard, choose a different set from the same row.

Workshop Menu			
Can I Do This?	▲ **Working On It!** I could use some extra help. *Jacob*	● **Getting It!** I just need some more practice. *Ana*	■ **Got It!** I'm ready for a challenge. *Nicholas*
Make trades with base-ten pieces.	**Play Make a Flat**	**Play Make a Flat** or **Play Make a Pack with Bits**	**Play Make a Pack with Bits**
Show a number different ways.	*Show Choco Packages* **Questions 1–5**	*Show Choco Packages* **Questions 3–6**	*Show Choco Packages* **Questions 6–8**
Compare large numbers.	*Compare the Number of Chocos* **Questions 1–5**	*Compare the Number of Chocos* **Questions 3–8**	*Compare the Number of Chocos* **Questions 6–9**

▲●■ Make a Flat

The object of the game is to be the first player to fill the flat. This is a game for two players.

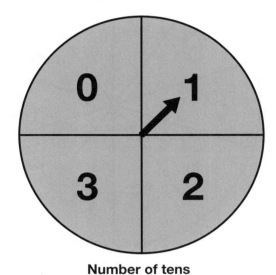

Number of tens   **Number of tens**

Materials

- 1 Make a Flat Game Board for each player
- 1 gray spinner with 0–3 for tens
- 1 white spinner with 0–9 for ones
- clear plastic spinner or pencil and paper clip
- 20 bits, 20 skinnies, and 1 flat

Directions

1. Spin the gray spinner once and take that many skinnies. Spin the white spinner once and take that many bits.

2. Line up your skinnies and bits on your game board.

3. Trade bits for skinnies according to the Fewest Pieces Rule.

4. After each turn, write the total number of base-ten pieces you have in the "Running Total" column.

5. Take turns repeating the steps above.

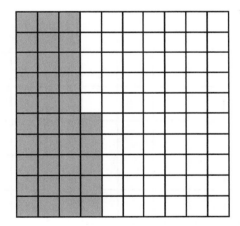

Turn	Running Total
1	23
2	35
3	
4	
5	
6	
7	

*A sample game board
after two spins*

Make a Flat Game Board

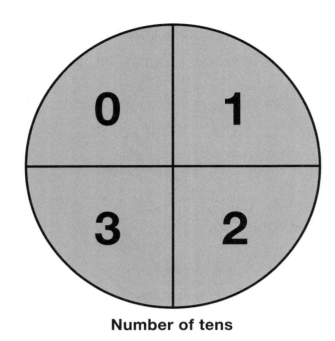

Number of tens

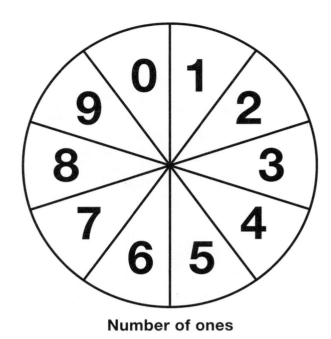

Number of ones

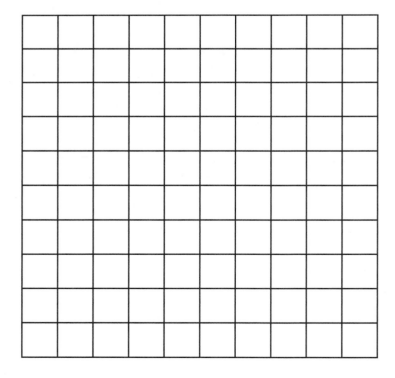

Turn	Running Total
1	
2	
3	
4	
5	
6	
7	
8	
9	
10	

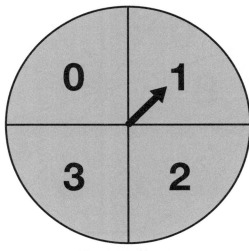 Make a Pack with Bits

The object of the game is to be the first player to complete a pack. This is a game for two players.

Number of hundreds   **Number of tens and ones**

Materials

- 1 Make a Pack with Bits Game Board for each player
- 1 gray spinner with 0–3 for hundreds
- 1 white spinner with 0–9 for tens and ones
- clear plastic spinner or pencil and paper clip
- 20 bits, 20 skinnies, 20 flats, and 1 pack

Directions

1. Spin the gray spinner once and take that many flats. Spin the white spinner once and take that many skinnies. Spin the white spinner again and take that many bits.

2. Stack up your flats, skinnies, and bits on your game board.

3. Trade pieces according to the Fewest Pieces Rule.

4. After each turn, write the total number of base-ten pieces you have in the "Running Total" column.

5. Take turns repeating the steps above.

Make a Pack with Bits Game Board

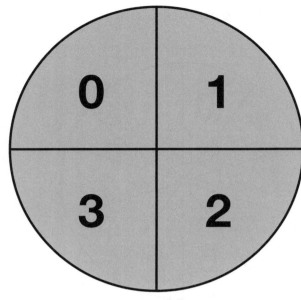

Number of hundreds

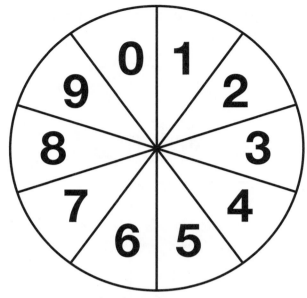

Number of tens and ones

Turn	Running Total
1	
2	
3	
4	
5	
6	
7	
8	
9	
10	

Name _____

Date _____

Show Choco Packages

At the TIMS Candy Company, Maya and Nikia are packaging Chocos. They do not always follow the Fewest Pieces Rule.

- For each row, find the number of Chocos Maya and Nikia packaged.
- If the number of Chocos is the same, use base-ten shorthand to show how to package them using the Fewest Pieces Rule. If they are not the same, write "not the same" in the Fewest Pieces column.

Maya's Count	Nikia's Count	Fewest Pieces
1. Number of Chocos: _____	 Number of Chocos: _____	
2. Number of Chocos: _____	 Number of Chocos: _____	

- For each row, find the number of Chocos Maya and Nikia packaged.
- If the number of Chocos is the same, use base-ten shorthand to show how to package them using the Fewest Pieces Rule. If they are not the same, write "not the same" in the Fewest Pieces column.

Maya's Count	Nikia's Count	Fewest Pieces
3. [icons] Number of Chocos: ____	[icons] Number of Chocos: ____	
4. [icons] Number of Chocos: ____	[icons] Number of Chocos: ____	

Workshop: Place Value

Name _____ Date _____

Use base-ten shorthand to show three different ways Maya and Nikia can package the number of Chocos in each row. Write a number sentence for each way. If a number sentence is given, sketch the base-ten pieces needed to match the partitions.

	Number	Fewest Pieces	Second Way	Third Way
5.	232	Number Sentence: $200 + 30 + 2 = 232$	Number Sentence: _____	Number Sentence: _____
6.	56	Number Sentence: _____	Number Sentence: _____	Number Sentence: $30 + 26 = 56$

Use base-ten shorthand to show three different ways Maya and Nikia can package the number of Chocos in each row. Write a number sentence for each way. If a number sentence is given, sketch the base-ten pieces needed to match the partitions.

Number	Fewest Pieces	Second Way	Third Way
7. ▪ 1435	Number Sentence:	Number Sentence: 1400 + 30 + 5 = 1435	Number Sentence:
8. ▪ 2067	Number Sentence:	Number Sentence:	Number Sentence: 1000 + 900 + 160 + 7 = ?

Compare the Number of Chocos

▲ ☐ ☐ **1.** **A.** Maya and Tom packaged Chocos. How many Chocos did each person package?

Maya's count _____   Tom's count _____

Maya	Tom
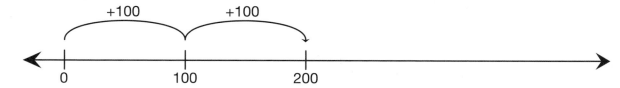	
Number sentence	Number sentence
_____	_____

B. Who packaged more?

Show or tell how you know.

C. Which worker showed his or her count using the Fewest Pieces Rule, Maya or Tom? Show or tell how you know.

D. Tom started to show the number of Chocos he counted on a number line. Help Tom finish.

+100   +100

0   100   200

▲ □ □ **2.** **A.** Nikia and Maruta packaged Chocos. How many Chocos did each person package?

Nikia's count _____   Maruta's count _____

Nikia	Maruta
Number sentence _____	Number sentence _____

B. Write a true number sentence that compares Nikia's count to Maruta's count using < or >.

_____

▲ ● □ **3.** Nikia and Maruta both like to write number sentences to show how they package Chocos. Use <, >, or = to make the number sentences true.

	Nikia		Maruta
A.	30 + 4	○	10 + 10 + 10 + 14
B.	200 + 100 + 70 + 1	○	300 + 70 + 1
C.	100 + 60 + 17	○	100 + 50 + 6
D.	900 + 8	○	1000 + 8

▲●☐ 4. Use base-ten shorthand to show how Nikia and Maruta packaged the Chocos in Question 3C.

Nikia	Maruta

▲●☐ 5. How many more Chocos did Nikia package than Maruta in Question 3C? Show or tell how you solved it. You may use the number line or solve it another way.

☐●■ 6. **A.** Maya and Nikia used number lines to show how many Chocos they packaged. Fill in the blanks below the number lines to show the hops.

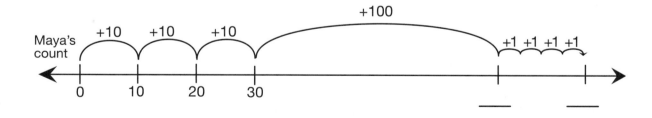

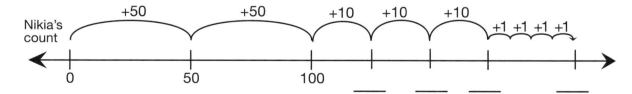

B. Who counted more? _____

Name _____ Date _____

Solve the following problems using the table.

Name	Chocos Packaged
Eric	33
Maya	61
Tom	107
Maruta	89

7. How many more Chocos did Maruta package than Maya? Show how to use the number line to solve this problem. Write a number sentence.

Number sentence: _____

8. Tom thinks he has packaged more Chocos than Eric and Maya put together. Is he right? Show or tell how you know.

9. Eric, Maya, Tom, and Maruta decided to put all the Chocos together. Use base-ten shorthand to show the number of Chocos they have altogether. Write a number sentence to show the total number of Chocos.

Number sentence: _____

Unit 5

Area of Different Shapes

Math Facts

Use the practice in this unit to review the subtraction facts in
Group 7 (14 − 7, 14 − 6, 14 − 8, 12 − 6, 12 − 7, 12 − 5, 10 − 5, 13 − 7, 13 − 6) and
Group 8 (15 − 7, 16 − 8, 17 − 8, 18 − 9, 18 − 10, 8 − 4, 7 − 4, 6 − 3, 15 − 8) and develop
number sense strategies for the multiplication facts for the square numbers.

Hours in a Day

What do you do during each hour of a day? Complete the table.
Use your individual clock to help you.

Time	Activity
12:00 AM (Midnight)	
1:00 AM	
2:00 AM	
12:00 PM (Noon)	
1:00 PM	
2:00 PM	

Broken Clocks

The minute hand is missing from these clocks. Decide the hour and then estimate the number of minutes past the hour. Use your individual clock to help you.

1.

_____

2.

_____

3.
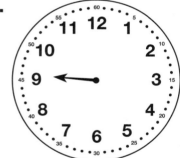

_____

4.

_____

5.

_____

6.

_____

Check-In: Questions 7–12

7.

_____

8.

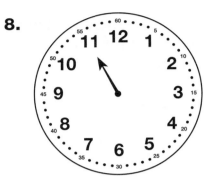

_____

9. Tell how you decided the time shown on the clock in Question 7.

10.

_____

11.

_____

12. Tell how you decided the time shown on the clock in Question 11.

Time to the Nearest Five Minutes

The Hour Hand at Home

Homework

Dear Family Member:

The class is learning to tell time. Today we focused on the hour hand. Help your child with the times described below the clock. For each clock, your child will show the position of the hour hand only.

Thank you.

Show the position of the hour hand for each time.

1.

I get up.

2.

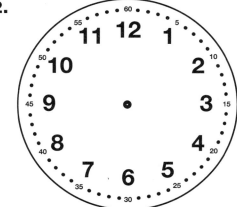

I leave for school.

3.

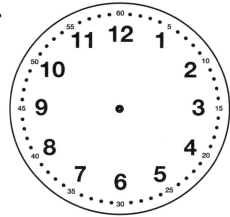

I get home.

4.

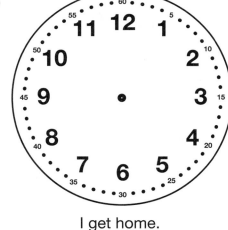

I eat dinner.

5.

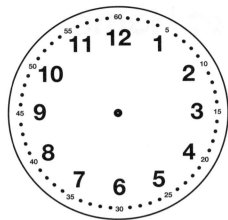

My favorite TV show begins.

6.

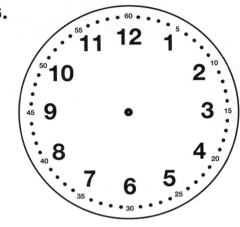

My favorite TV show ends.

7.

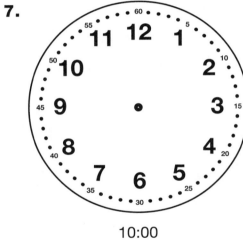

10:00

8.

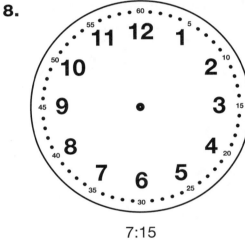

7:15

9.

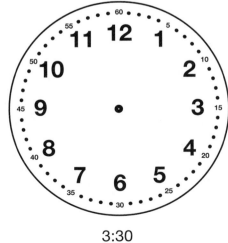

3:30

10.

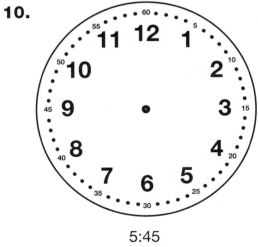

5:45

Time around the Clock

Write or draw the times on the clocks below.

1.

_____ 10:25 _____

2.
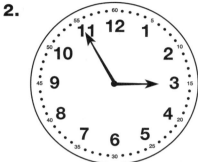
_____

3.
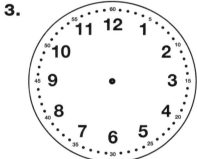
_____ 7:45 _____

4.

_____

5.

_____

6.
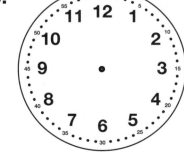
_____ 4:30 _____

Time to the Nearest Five Minutes

7.

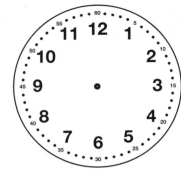

1:30
_____

8.

_____

9.

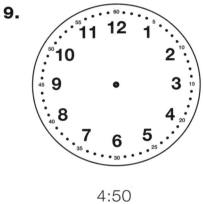

4:50
_____

10.

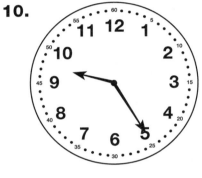

_____

11.

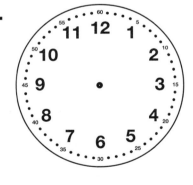

7:15
_____

12.

_____

Elapsed Time

Draw the hands on the clocks to show the start time and stop time for each student's activity. Then find the time that elapsed during the activity. Give the elapsed time in hours and minutes.

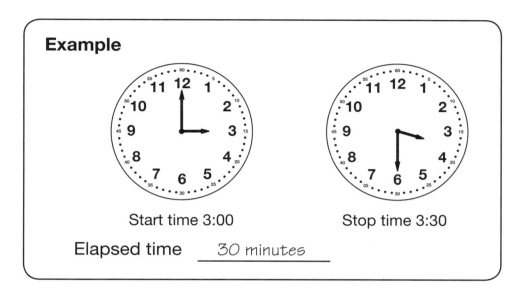

Example

Start time 3:00   Stop time 3:30

Elapsed time   _30 minutes_

1. Roberto's homework

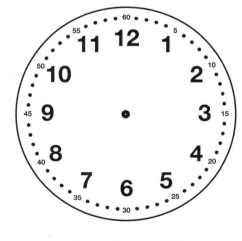 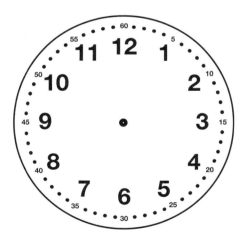

Start time 4:30   Stop time 6:30

Elapsed time _____

2. Shannon's band practice

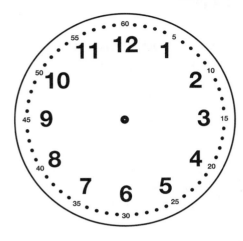

Start time 3:30

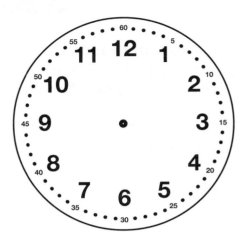

Stop time 5:00

Elapsed time _____

3. Jerome's babysitting

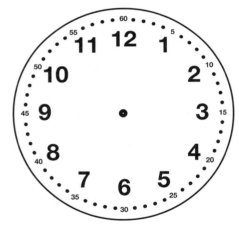

Start time 1:00

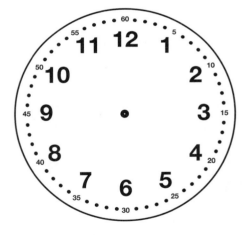

Stop time 2:15

Elapsed time _____

Name _____ Date _____

Show the start time, stop time and the elapsed times for each of the following situations.

4. Irma and Nila started practicing their song for the school concert at 3:30. They finished practicing at 5:00.

Start Time   Stop Time

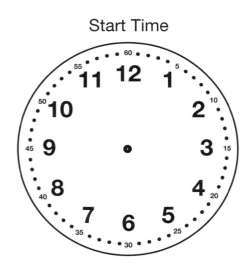

Elapsed time _____

5. Keenya and John started decorating cookies at 9:00. They decorated the last cookie at 10:45.

Start Time   Stop Time

Elapsed time _____

Time to the Nearest Five Minutes   **SAB • Grade 3 • Unit 5 • Lesson 1**

6. When Nicholas finished his math homework at 6:00 he said it took him too long to do it. He started at 5:30. How long did it take him to do his homework? Show or tell how you decided.

7. Mark started riding his bike at 3:00. He finished his ride at 4:15. How long did Mark ride his bike?

8. Jason said he practiced his violin for 25 minutes. If he started practicing at 4:15 what time did he finish?

9. A. Liz started reading her book at 6:30. The clock shows the time when she finished reading. How long did Liz read?

B. Show or tell how you found the answer to Question 9A.

Check Each Other

1. Find the area in square centimeters.

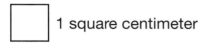 1 square centimeter

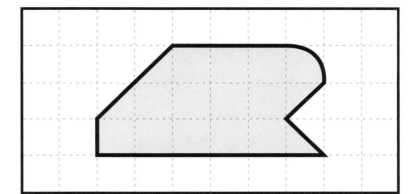

Area _____

2. Luis and Grace each found the area of the shape in Question 1. Look at their work.

Luis's Work

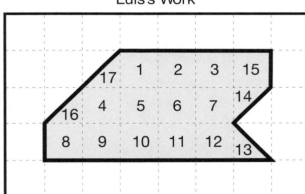

The area is about
17 square centimaters.

Grace's Work

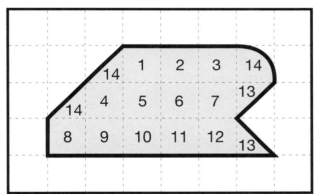

The area is about
14 square centimeters.

A. Do you agree with these students? Why or why not?

B. How can Luis improve his work?

C. How can Grace improve her work?

Area of Five Shapes

Homework

Find the area of each of the shapes on the grid below.

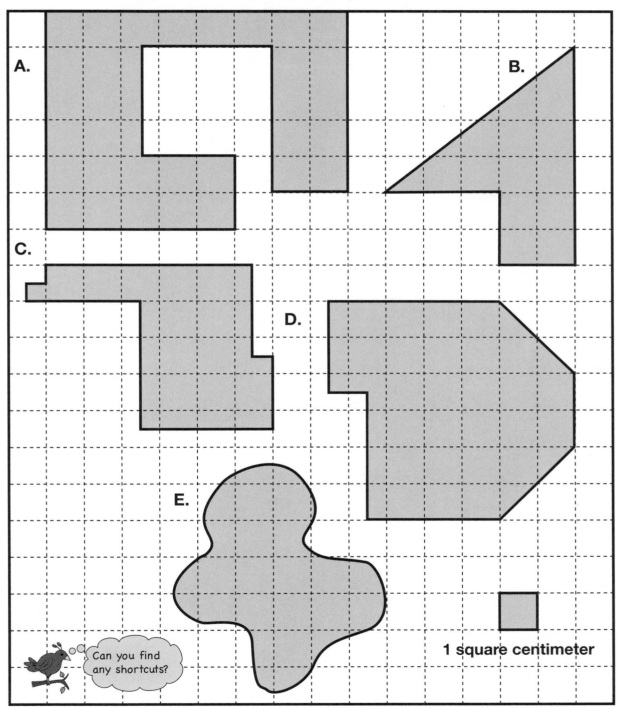

A.

B.

C.

D.

E.

Can you find any shortcuts?

1 square centimeter

Boo the Blob Changes Shape

Boo the Blob is a very special creature who is completely flat. He tries to trick his friends by changing his shape. His friends always know who he is because he cannot change his area.

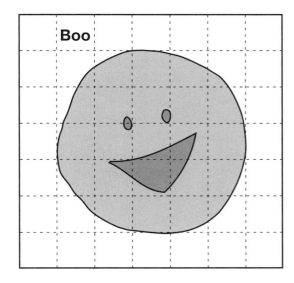

One of the three blobs below is Boo in another form. Can you find him? Which one is he?

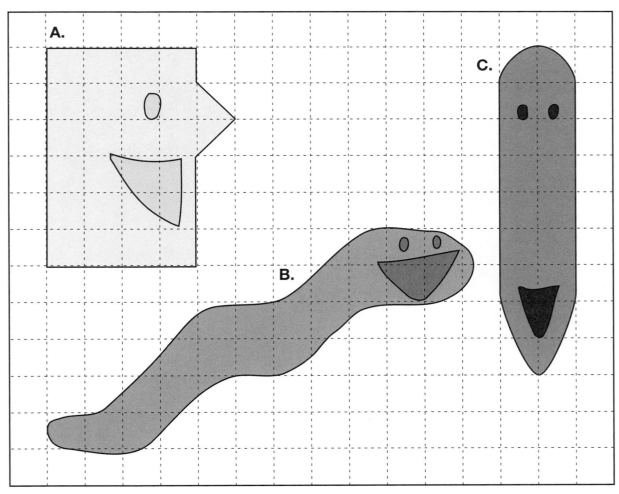

Name _____ Date _____

Record the area you counted for Shapes A, B, and C in the data table. Record and compare data from two classmates as well. Do not write anything in the column labeled "Median" or the last row yet.

Shape vs. Area

Shape	Area (in square centimeters)			
	My Data	Classmate #1	Classmate #2	Median
A				
B				
C				

1. List the three areas your group found for Shape A in order from smallest to largest. Circle the middle value.

2. The middle value is the **median**. Record the median area for Shape A in the data table.

3. Record the median values for Shapes B and C in the data table.

4. Which shape is Boo? Explain how you decided.

Check-In: Questions 5–9

5. Draw Boo the Blob as a different shape. Use the Centimeter Grid below. Label this Shape D.

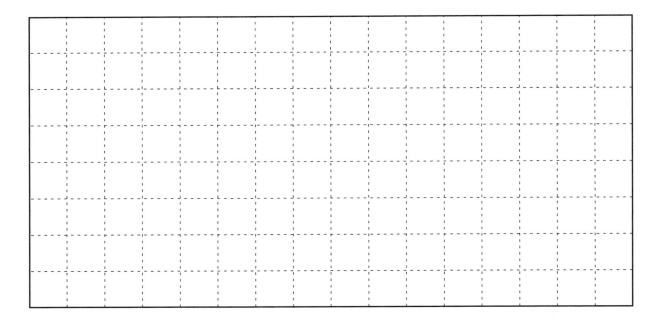

6. Find the area of Shape D. Record the area in the Shape vs. Area data table.

7. Trade papers with two classmates. Ask each of them to also find the area of Shape D and record their measurements in the Shape vs. Area data table.

8. Find the median area for Shape D.

9. Did you draw Boo the Blob as a new shape? Explain how you decided.

Name _____

Date _____

Boo the Blob Changes Shape
Check-In: Questions 5–9
Feedback Box

Expectation			Check In	Comments
Recognize that different shapes can have the same area. [Q# 5]	E1			
Find the area of shapes with straight or curved sides by counting square units. [Q# 6–7]	E3			
Find the median of a data set. [Q# 8]	E7			

Yes . . .	Yes, but . . .	No, but . . .	No . . .
MPE5. Show my work. I show or tell how I arrived at my answer so someone else can understand my thinking. [Q# 9]			
MPE6. Use labels. I use labels to show what numbers mean. [Q# 9]			

Name _____ Date _____

Name the Blob

_____ the Blob is a special creature who is
Name

completely flat. _____ area is always
His or Her

_____ square centimeters.

Draw _____ **the Blob as two different shapes.**
Name

Use the Centimeter Grid below.

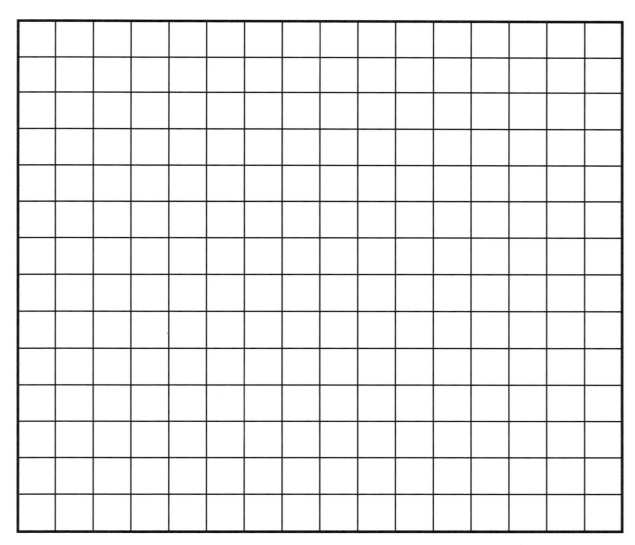

The Better "Picker Upper" Lab

Draw a picture of what you are going to do to compare paper towel brands. Label the variables in your picture.

1. What variables will you study in this lab?

2. What variables should be fixed or should not change in this lab? Tell why.

Collect

3. Work with your partners to do the lab and record your data on the data table.
- Label each brand of paper towel.
- Put your name on the paper towels.

Area of Spot vs. Brand of Paper Towel

T Brand of Paper Towel	*A* Area of Spot (in _____)			
	Trial 1	Trial 2	Trial 3	Median

Graph

4. Graph the median area for each brand of paper towel on *Centimeter Graph Paper*.
- Label the horizontal axis Brand of Paper Towel (*T*).
- Label the vertical axis Area of Spot (*A*). Include the units.
- Choose an appropriate scale for the vertical axis.
- Title the graph "Area of Spot."

Use your graph to find answers to the following questions.

5. Which paper towel had the spot with the largest area? What was the area of the spot?

6. Which paper towel had the spot with the smallest area? What was the area of the spot?

7. How much larger was the largest spot than the smallest spot? Explain how you found your answer.

8. How would the graph look if you dropped twice as many drops on each paper towel?

9. Look at your graph. Which towel do you think picks up the most water? Show or tell how you decided.

10. Professor Peabody decided that Brand C is the better "picker upper" or the one that picks up the most water. Do you agree with Professor Peabody? Why or why not?

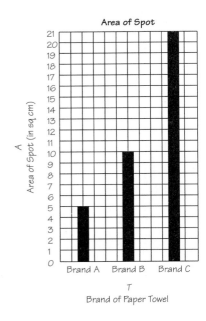

Area of Spot

Area of Spot (in sq cm)

Brand A   Brand B   Brand C

Brand of Paper Towel

I think Brand C will pick up the most water because it had the spot with the largest area.

Professor Peabody Makes Another Model

After looking at the area of the spots made, Professor Peabody was still not sure which paper towel was the better "picker upper." He decided to make a different model. He went back to his data to make a new model.

The better "picker upper" will hold more drops of water!

This brand will hold 30 drops of water.

median area

Brand A

5   5   5

5   5   5

Collect

11. Work with your partners to find out how many drops of water each brand of paper towel can pick up.

For each brand:
- Label a sheet of copy paper with the paper towel brand's name.
- Choose the median paper towel spot.
- Trace the median spot onto the sheet of paper as many times as it will fit.
- Find the number of drops that can be picked up by each brand of towel.
- Record the data on the data table below.

Number of Drops vs. Brand of Paper Towel

T Brand of Paper Towel	N Number of Drops

Graph

12. Graph your data on a piece of *Centimeter Graph Paper*.
- Label the horizontal axis Brand of Paper Towel (T).
- Label the vertical axis Number of Drops (N), include units.
- Choose an appropriate scale for the vertical axis.
- Title the graph "Number of Drops."

13. Which brand of paper towel had the tallest bar on your Number of Drops graph?

14. Did this same brand of paper towel have the tallest bar on your Area of Spot graph? Predict why.

15. Professor Peabody made the models below to compare the paper towel brands. He traced the spots on a full sheet of each brand of paper towel.

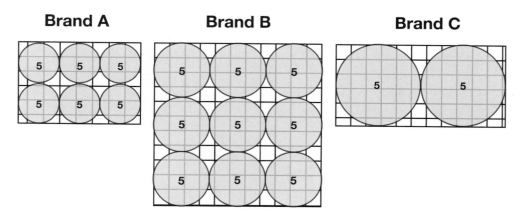

He graphed the number of drops that each paper towel could pick up.

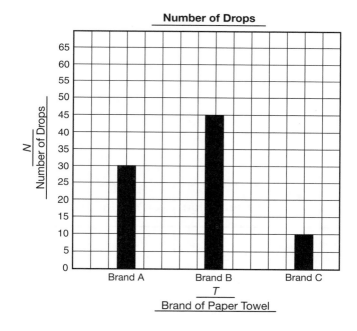

He decided the Brand B was the better "picker upper" because the paper towel could hold the most drops of water.

Do you agree with Professor Peabody? Why or why not?

16. Compare your graphs and diagrams. Which towel do you think is the better "picker upper"? Show or tell how you decided.

The Better "Picker Upper" Lab Feedback Box	Expectation	Check In	Comments
Find the area of shapes with curved sides by counting square centimeters. [Q# 3]]	E3		
Make a scaled bar graph using numerical data. [Q# 4 and 12]	E5		
Read a graph to find information about a data set. [Q# 5–7 and 13–14]	E6		
Find the median of a data set. [Q# 3]	E7		
Make predictions and generalizations about a data set using data tables, graphs, and diagrams. [Q# 8–10 and 15–16]	E8		

Name _____ Date _____

Haunted House Footprint

Do you think you would have been a suspect in the story? Trace your footprint on the grid and answer the following questions.

1. What is the area of your footprint in square centimeters?

Area: _____

2. What is the length of your footprint in centimeters?

Length: _____

3. The area of the mystery footprint is approximately 53 square centimeters. Its length is 15 centimeters. Do you think you would have been a suspect in *The Haunted House* mystery? Why or why not?

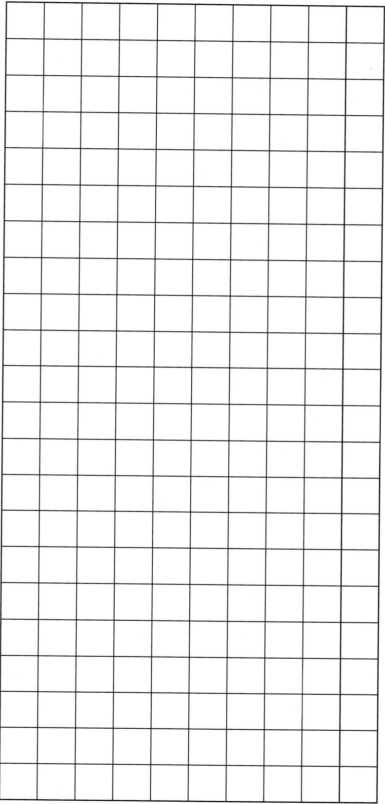

Haunted House Footprint Feedback Box

Expectation	Check In	Comments
Find the area of shapes with curved sides by counting square units. [Q# 1]	E3	
Make generalizations about a data set using a data table. [Q# 3]	E8	

	Yes . . .	Yes, but . . .	No, but . . .	No . . .
MPE5. Show my work. I show or tell how I arrived at my answer so someone else can understand my thinking. [Q# 1–3]				
MPE6. Use labels. I use labels to show what numbers mean. [Q# 1–3]				

The Haunted House

Unit 6

Adding Larger Numbers

Math Facts
Use the practice in this unit to review the subtraction facts in all groups and develop strategies for solving the multiplication facts for the 9s.

Use Tens and Ones

Julia's Strategy for 28 + 44:

$$28 = 20 + 8$$
$$+ \; 44 = 40 + 4$$
$$\overline{ \; 60 + 12 = 72}$$

1. Solve each problem using Julia's strategy.

A. $41 =$
    $+ \; 36 =$

B. $33 =$
    $+ \; 57 =$

C. $57 =$
    $+ \; 26 =$

D. $38 =$
    $+ \; 67 =$

E. $79 =$
    $+ \; 26 =$

F. $84 =$
    $+ \; 19 =$

Chris's Strategy for 28 + 44:

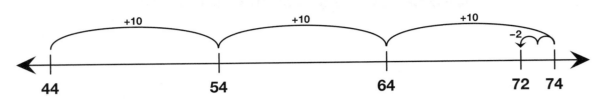

Chris's Number Sentence: 44 + 30 − 2 = 72

2. Solve each problem using Chris's strategy or another number line strategy.

A. 37 + 49

Number Sentence: _____

B. 69 + 26

Number Sentence: _____

C. 138 + 27

Number Sentence: _____

D. 84 + 19

Number Sentence: _____

Check-In: Questions 3–5

3. Show how to solve each problem using Julia's strategy, a number line strategy, or another mental math strategy. Use each strategy at least once.

A.   47
       + 35
       ――――

B.   29
       + 54
       ――――

C. 36 + 26 =

D. 136 + 74 =

E. 89 + 51 =

4. Chris and Julia each showed how they solved 28 + 32.
Compare their strategies.

Chris's strategy: Julia's strategy:

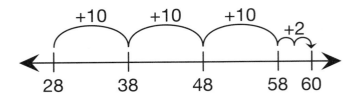

$$28 = 20 + 8$$
$$+\ 32 = 30 + 2$$
$$\overline{\qquad\qquad 50 + 10 = 60}$$

How are they the same? How are they different?

5. Look at your solutions to the problems in Question 3. Which strategy
do you like best? Why?

Use Tens and Ones Check-In: Questions 3–5 Feedback Box	Expectation	Check-in	Comments
Use place value concepts to make connections among representations. [Q# 3 and 4]	E1		
Represent and solve addition problems using number lines. [Q# 3]	E2		
Add using mental math strategies. [Q# 3]	E3		
Add using expanded form. [Q# 3]	E4		

Standard and Expanded Form

Homework

1. Write the following numbers in standard form. Standard form is a "regular number."

   A.  _____

   B. _____

   C.  _____

   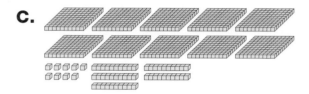

2. Put the numbers from Question 1 in order from least to greatest.

   _____ _____ _____

3. Write the following numbers in standard form.

   A. 600 + 80 + 2 _____

   B. 5000 + 200 + 4 _____

   C. 3000 + 900 + 6 _____

4. Put the numbers from Question 3 in order from least to greatest.

   _____ _____ _____

5. Write the following numbers in expanded form. The first one is done for you.

A. 4361   _____*4000 + 300 + 60 + 1*_____

B. 2092   _____

C. 8056   _____

D. 950   _____

6. Put the numbers from Question 5 in order from least to greatest.

_____   _____   _____   _____

7. Write the following numbers in standard form.

A.    _____

B. 200 + 90 + 6   _____

C. 300 + 40 + 0   _____

D. _____

8. Put the numbers from Question 7 in order from least to greatest.

_____   _____   _____   _____

Hundreds Template

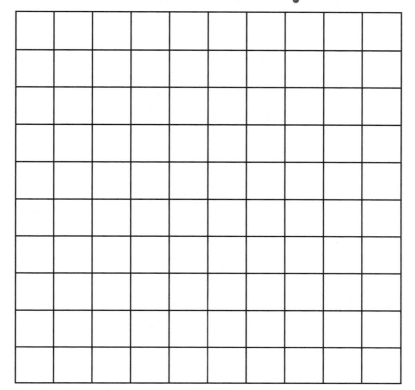

Hundreds Template

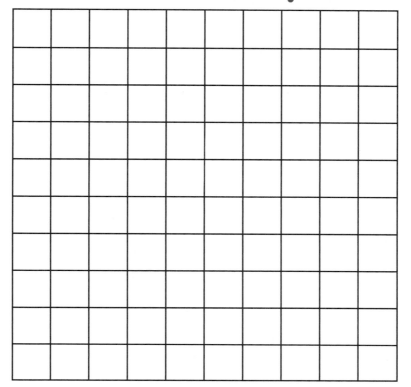

Name _____

Date _____

Rounding Numbers

1. Place these numbers on the number line:
87, 36, 25, 160, 150, 112, 198, 102, 7, 177

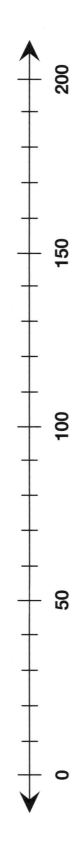

| 0 | 50 | 100 | 150 | 200 |

2. For each number, give the closest ten and hundred. The first one is done for you.

	Number	Closest 10	Closest 100
A.	87	90	100
B.	36		
C.	25		
D.	160		
E.	150		

	Number	Closest 10	Closest 100
F.	112		
G.	198		
H.	102		
I.	7		
J.	177		

3. For each number, give the closest ten and the closest hundred. The first one is done for you. You can use base-ten pieces or think of a number line.

	Number	**Closest 10**	**Closest 100**
A.	284	280	300
B.	128		
C.	421		
D.	910		
E.	203		
F.	85		
G.	550		
H.	805		
I.	369		
J.	1502		

Name _____

Date _____

Homework

1. Place these numbers on the number line:
228, 309, 299, 72, 240, 391, 349, 214, 150, 191

| 0 | 50 | 100 | 150 | 200 | 250 | 300 | 350 | 400 |

2. For each number, give the closest ten and hundred. The first one is done for you.

	Number	Closest 10	Closest 100
A.	228	230	200
B.	309		
C.	299		
D.	72		
E.	240		

	Number	Closest 10	Closest 100
F.	391		
G.	349		
H.	214		
I.	150		
J.	191		

Connect Addition Methods

Use mental math strategies to estimate the sums. Then solve each of the addition problems using base-ten pieces. Finally, solve the problems using a paper-and-pencil method.

1.

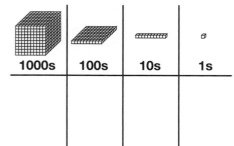

1000s	100s	10s	1s

$$\begin{array}{r} 17 \\ + 32 \\ \hline \end{array}$$

2.

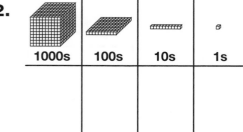

1000s	100s	10s	1s

$$\begin{array}{r} 27 \\ + 35 \\ \hline \end{array}$$

3.

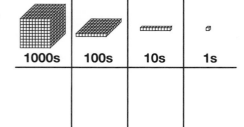

1000s	100s	10s	1s

$$\begin{array}{r} 83 \\ + 32 \\ \hline \end{array}$$

4.

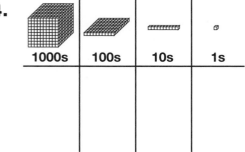

1000s	100s	10s	1s

$$\begin{array}{r} 26 \\ 66 \\ + 18 \\ \hline \end{array}$$

Tara, Julia, Yolanda, and Josh started the problems below. Before they could finish, the fire alarm rang. Help the students finish the problems using the method they chose.

5. | 64 + 28 = |

Tara's method:

$$64 = 60 + 4$$
$$+ 28 = \underline{\hspace{1cm}}$$

6. | 64 + 28 = |

Julia's method:

```
  64
+ 28
————
   2
```

7. | 44 + 29 = |

Yolanda's method:

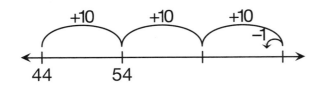

Number Sentence _____

8. | 44 + 29 = |

Josh's method:

```
  44
+ 29
————
  60
+ ____
```

Name _____

Date _____

Addition Strategies Menu

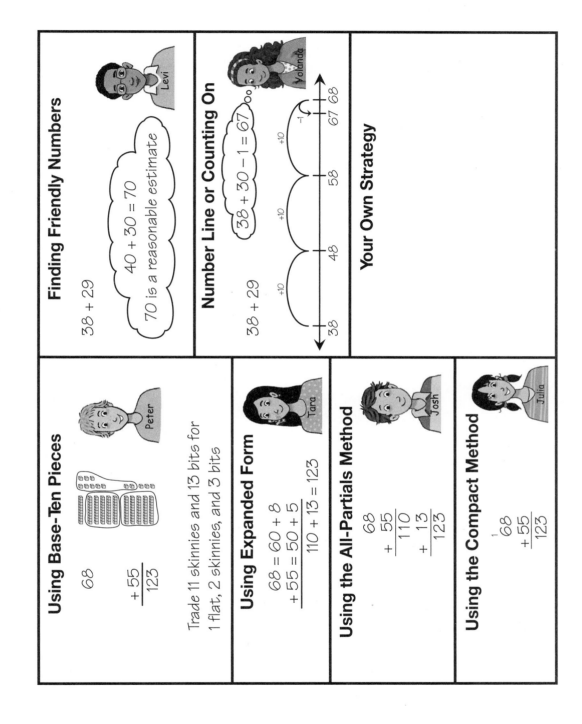

Finding Friendly Numbers

38 + 29

40 + 30 = 70

70 is a reasonable estimate

Levi

Number Line or Counting On

38 + 29

38 + 30 − 1 = 67

Yolanda

Your Own Strategy

Using Base-Ten Pieces

68
+ 55
___
123

Trade 11 skinnies and 13 bits for
1 flat, 2 skinnies, and 3 bits

Peter

Using Expanded Form

68 = 60 + 8
+ 55 = 50 + 5
_____
110 + 13 = 123

Tara

Using the All-Partials Method

68
+ 55
____
110
+ 13
____
123

Josh

Using the Compact Method

¹
68
+ 55
____
123

Julia

Using Addition Strategies

Solve the problems in two ways. You may use base-ten shorthand to show how to use base-ten pieces, a pencil-and-paper method, or your own method. Use the *Addition Strategies Menu* from the *Student Activity Book*.

1. $53 + 40 =$

2. $\begin{array}{r} 27 \\ + 41 \\ \hline \end{array}$

3. $98 + 50 =$

4. $\begin{array}{r} 36 \\ + 57 \\ \hline \end{array}$

5.   38
    + 42

6. 77 + 18 =

7.   12
    35
  + 45

8. 40 + 82 =

Adding with Base-Ten Pieces

Nikia and Maruta both work at the TIMS Candy Company. Nikia made 196 Chocos. Maruta made 232 Chocos. They used base-ten pieces to figure out how much candy they made together. They recorded their work with base-ten shorthand and a recording sheet.

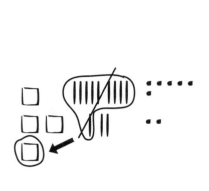

1000s	100s	10s	1s
	1	9	6
+	2	3	2
	3	12	8
	4	2	8

Fewest Pieces

1. Another time Nikia made 237 Chocos and Maruta made 155. Find how much they made altogether. Solve the problem using base-ten shorthand and record your work on the recording sheet. Make sure you use the Fewest Pieces Rule.

1000s	100s	10s	1s

Name _____ Date _____

Solve the problems using base-ten shorthand. Then record your work on the recording sheet.

2. 69 + 23 + 18

1000s	100s	10s	1s

3. 324 + 194

1000s	100s	10s	1s

4. 2607 + 748

1000s	100s	10s	1s

5. 1308 + 4196

1000s	100s	10s	1s

Addition with Larger Numbers

Digits Game

The object of the game is to get the largest correct answer to an addition problem. Any number of people can play.

Materials

- one set of *Digit Cards 0–9*
- paper and pencils

Directions

1. One person is the leader, and the others are players. The leader chooses and draws one playing board so that all of the players can see it.

 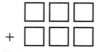 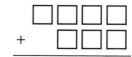

2. Each player draws the playing board on his or her paper.

3. The leader shuffles the cards, places them face down, picks the top card, and reads the digit to all the players.

4. Each player writes that digit in one of the boxes on his or her playing board. Each player must decide where to place the digit in order to get the largest answer. Once a player has written down a digit, it may not be moved. No digit will be repeated.

5. The leader places the first card in a discard pile, then reads the next card. Players place this digit in another unfilled box. Play continues until all the boxes are filled.

6. When all the boxes are filled, players add to find their answers. Since the player with the largest **correct** answer wins the game, players should check their answers using a second strategy or estimate to see if their answers are reasonable.

Variation

The leader decides if the largest or smallest correct answer wins the game.

Problem Solving

Solve the problems. Use the *Addition Strategies Menu* in the *Student Guide* Reference section.

1. Romesh and Jason are playing the Digits Game. After four cards, their boards are below. Find each boy's sum using two different methods.

   Romesh   Second Method

   Jason

   ```
     7 4
   + 8 6
   ```

2. Kathy and Sara played a game for the largest number. Their boards are below. Find each sum. Explain a strategy for deciding if your answers are reasonable.

   Kathy   Estimation Strategy

   ```
     8 1 4
   + 6 2 3
   ```

   Sara

   ```
     1 6 3
   + 8 4 2
   ```

3. Who won Kathy and Sara's game? Show how you decided who had the largest number.

4. Miguel's game board looks like the one below. He is trying to find the largest sum. The next card is a 5. Where should he put the 5? Explain your thinking.

```
  [ ] [6] [1]
+ [7] [ ] [4]
```

✔ Check-In: Question 5

5. Miguel's completed game board is to the right. He used the all-partials method to find the sum.

```
  [9] [6] [1]
+ [7] [5] [4]
─────────────
  1  6  0  0
           1  1
+             5
─────────────
  1  6  1  6
```

A. Explain an estimation strategy for checking if his answer is reasonable.

B. Check Miguel's calculations. Do you agree with his solution? Why or why not?

Adding the Parts

Solve the problems using any method. Use the *Addition Strategies Menu* in the Reference section of the *Student Guide*. Check to see if your answer is reasonable.

Johnny solved this problem using the All-Partials Method:

$$\begin{array}{r} 574 \\ + 859 \\ \hline 1300 \\ 120 \\ +\ \ 13 \\ \hline 1433 \end{array}$$

Suzanne solved it using Expanded Form:

$$\begin{array}{rcrcccc} 574 &=& 500 &+& 70 &+& 4 \\ + 859 &=& 800 &+& 50 &+& 9 \\ \hline && 1300 &+& 120 &+& 13 = 1433 \end{array}$$

A.
$$\begin{array}{r} 148 \\ + 754 \\ \hline \end{array}$$

B.
$$\begin{array}{r} 652 \\ + 283 \\ \hline \end{array}$$

C.
$$\begin{array}{r} 143 \\ + 629 \\ \hline \end{array}$$

D.
$$\begin{array}{r} 162 \\ + 575 \\ \hline \end{array}$$

E.   153
        + 479
        _____

F.   342
        + 568
        _____

G.   159
        + 456
        _____

H.   678
        + 543
        _____

I. Show how Question A can be solved using a mental math strategy.

J. Explain an estimation strategy that shows your answer to Question H is reasonable.

Palindrome Recording Chart

Choose a color for each kind of palindrome. Find and color each kind in the chart.

	palindrome		1 step		2 step		3 step

	4 step		5 step		6 step

0	1	2	3	4	5	6	7	8	9
10	11	12	13	14	15	16	17	18	19
20	21	22	23	24	25	26	27	28	29
30	31	32	33	34	35	36	37	38	39
40	41	42	43	44	45	46	47	48	49
50	51	52	53	54	55	56	57	58	59
60	61	62	63	64	65	66	67	68	69
70	71	72	73	74	75	76	77	78	79
80	81	82	83	84	85	86	87	88	89
90	91	92	93	94	95	96	97	98	99

Palindromes and Addition Practice

Solve the following problems. Be prepared to show or tell your strategy.

- **Which problems can you solve in your head?**
- **Which problems can you solve by sketching a number line or a few quick notes?**
- **Which problems do you need to use pencil and paper to solve?**

A. 19 + 91

B. 64 + 46

C. 12 + 21

D. 97 + 79

E. 45 + 54

F. 31 + 13

G. Choose one problem and show how you used a mental math strategy.

H. Choose one problem and show how you used a paper-and-pencil method.

Workshop: Addition

Name _____

Date _____

Addition Strategies Menu

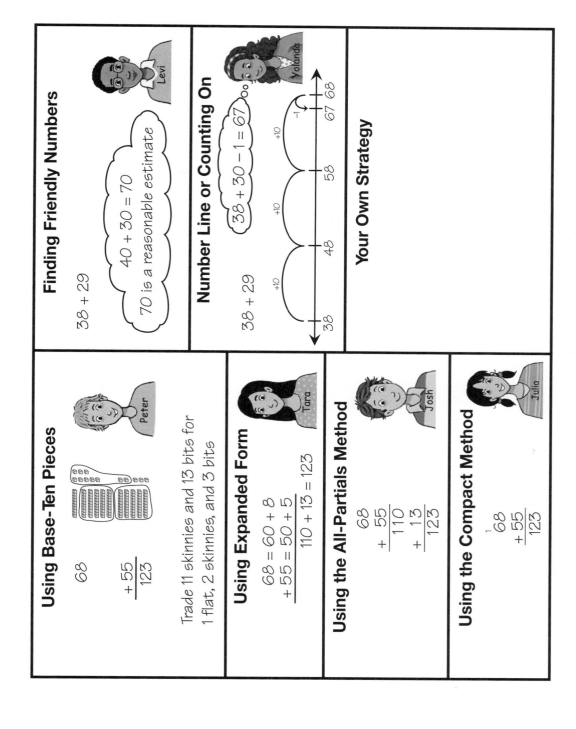

Finding Friendly Numbers

Levi

38 + 29

40 + 30 = 70

70 is a reasonable estimate

Number Line or Counting On

Yolanda

38 + 29

38 + 30 − 1 = 67

+10   +10   +10   −1

38   48   58   67 68

Your Own Strategy

Using Base-Ten Pieces

Peter

```
   68
 + 55
  123
```

Trade 11 skinnies and 13 bits for
1 flat, 2 skinnies, and 3 bits.

Using Expanded Form

Tara

```
68 = 60 + 8
+ 55 = 50 + 5
     110 + 13 = 123
```

Using the All-Partials Method

Josh

```
   68
 + 55
  110
 + 13
  123
```

Using the Compact Method

Julia

```
    1
   68
 + 55
  123
```

Name _____   Date _____

Strategies to Add

Using Base-Ten Pieces

 **Self-Check: Question 1**

1. Solve 26 + 13 using base-ten pieces. Record your work with base-ten shorthand and the recording sheet.

1000s	100s	10s	1s	Number Sentences

Use the Workshop Menu to choose practice with using base-ten pieces.

Workshop Menu			
Can I Do This?	▲ **Working On It!** I could use some extra help. *Lee Yah*	● **Getting It!** I just need some more practice. *Roberto*	■ **Got It!** I'm ready for a challenge. *Michael*
Use the base-ten pieces to add.	**Questions 2–4, 8–9**	**Questions 4–9**	**Questions 4, 6–9**

Solve using base-ten pieces. Record your work with base-ten shorthand and the recording sheet.

▲☐☐ **2.** 27 + 32

1000s	100s	10s	1s	Number Sentences

▲☐☐ **3.** 68
        + 22

1000s	100s	10s	1s	Number Sentences

▲●■ **4.** 154
        + 28

1000s	100s	10s	1s	Number Sentences

5.   318
        + 455

1000s	100s	10s	1s	Number Sentences

6.   297
        + 88

1000s	100s	10s	1s	Number Sentences

7.   686 + 587

1000s	100s	10s	1s	Number Sentences

▲●■ **8.** Look at Tara's solution to 154 + 28.

I thought about base-ten pieces.

▢ ||||| ••••
    || •••••

100 + 50 + 20 + 4 + 8 = 182

This is a lot like using expanded form.

Tara

Tara thinks her strategy is similar to using expanded form.

$$
\begin{array}{r}
154 \\
+\ 28 \\
\hline
\end{array}
\begin{array}{l}
=\ 100 + 50 + 4 \\
20 + 8 \\
\hline
100 + 70 + 12 = 182
\end{array}
$$

Do you agree with Tara? Why or why not?

▲●■ **9.** Choose a problem from Questions 1–7 to solve using expanded form. Show your work below.

Name _____ Date _____

Using Mental Math Strategies

 Self-Check: Questions 10–11

10. Use a mental math strategy to solve 64 + 59. Explain your strategy.

11. Use a number line to show how to solve 458 + 302.

Use the Workshop Menu to choose practice with using mental math strategies to add.

Workshop Menu			
Can I Do This?	▲ **Working On It!** I could use some extra help. Roberto	● **Getting It!** I just need some more practice. Michael	■ **Got It!** I'm ready for a challenge. Lee Yah
Use mental math strategies to add.	Questions 12–14, 15E–G	Questions 13–15	Questions 14–15

▲ ☐ ☐ 12. Ms. Alfonso challenged the class to use a mental math strategy to solve each of the problems below. Grace and her classmates recorded their mental math strategies. Solve the problem next to each one using a similar strategy. Explain your thinking to your partner.

341 + 99 =

"I took the 1 from the 341 and put it with the 99 right away. Now the problem is 340 + 100, which is easy, 440."

Grace

A. 132 + 98 =

157 + 25=

"I thought about money."

150 + 25 = 175 + 7 = 182

Peter

B. 504 + 75 =

Ana

328 + 50 =

"I made notes, but I pictured the number line to count on. I started at 328 and hopped +2 to 330. It is easier to hop on tens. After five +10 hops I land on 380. Hop back 2 to 378. 328 + 50 = 378."

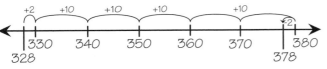

328 | 330 | 340 | 350 | 360 | 370 | 380
378

C. 352 + 98 =

220 + 160 =

"I separated out the hundreds. I added 200 + 100. That is 300. Then 20 + 60 = 80, so my answer is 300 + 80 = 380."

Frank

200 + 20
100 + 60
_____
300 + 80

D. 350 + 250 =

▲●▢ **13.** Use a mental math strategy to solve 548 + 132. Explain your strategy to your partner. Make some notes to record your partner's strategy below. Include your partner's name.

▲●■ **14.** Use a mental math strategy to solve 732 + 198. Explain your strategy to your partner. Make some notes to record your partner's strategy below. Include your partner's name.

15. Solve the following problems using a mental math strategy. Record your answer and explain your strategy to your partner. You do not need to write your strategy down, but you can jot down some notes.

⬜◼|●|◼ **A.** 325 + 175 =   ⬜|●|◼ **B.** 604 + 498 =

⬜|●|◼ **C.** 130 + 208 =   ⬜|●|◼ **D.** 849 + 121 =

▲|●|◼ **E.** 747 + 297 =   ▲|●|◼ **F.** 998 + 767 =

▲|●|◼ **G.** Show how you solved one of the problems above by describing your strategy in the thought bubble below.

Using Mental Math Strategies

 Self-Check: Question 16

Use the *Addition Strategies Menu*.

16. Solve 48 + 37 using three different strategies or methods.

Use the Workshop menu to choose practice with addition methods.

Workshop Menu			
Can I Do This?	▲ **Working On It!** I could use some extra help. Nicholas	● **Getting It!** I just need some more practice. Jacob	■ **Got It!** I'm ready for a challenge. Ana
Use different methods to add multidigit numbers.	**Questions 17–20** Use each of these methods at least once: • base-ten pieces • expanded form • all-partials	**Questions 20–21** Use each of these methods at least once: • all-partials • expanded form • compact method	**Questions 20–21** Use each of these methods at least once: • all-partials • compact method

△ ☐ ☐ 17. Here is how Sam solved
343 + 276.

Use the same method to solve
83 + 738.

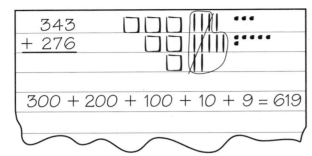

$$300 + 200 + 100 + 10 + 9 = 619$$

△ ☐ ☐ 18. Here is how Nisha solved
328 + 172.

Use the same method to solve
473 + 279.

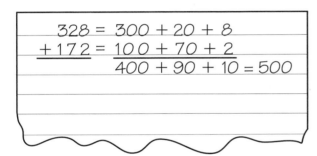

$$328 = 300 + 20 + 8$$
$$+172 = 100 + 70 + 2$$
$$400 + 90 + 10 = 500$$

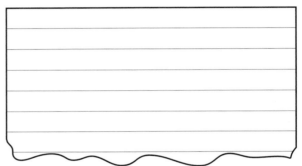

△ ☐ ☐ 19. Here is how Josh solved
329 + 476.

Use the same method to solve
847 + 278.

$$329$$
$$+ 476$$
$$700$$
$$90$$
$$15$$
$$805$$

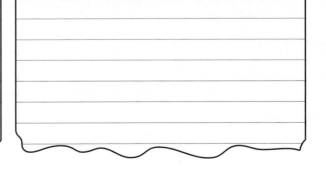

Workshop: Addition

▲●■20. Use the Workshop Menu to choose your own strategies and methods to solve the following problems. Use the *Addition Strategies Menu* as a guide.

A. 137 + 68

B.   66
        + 46

C. 35 + 46

D. 446 + 210

E. 232 + 124

F.   1448
       +2436

G.   23
        + 46

H. 2558 + 3226

Name _____   Date _____

■●■ 21. • Using the *Addition Strategies Menu* as a guide, show how to solve each problem using two different strategies. Compare your strategies. Circle the one you like best.

   • Use a mental math strategy at least three times.

   • Use each paper-and-pencil strategy at least once.

One Strategy	Another Strategy
A. 375 + 427 =	
B. 498 + 204 =	
C. 127 + 786	
D. 366 + 252	

Did you try all of the strategies on the *Addition Strategies Menu*?

Workshop: Addition

Unit 7

Subtracting Larger Numbers

	Practice	
	Daily Practice and Problems	**Home Practice**
Lesson 1: Time Again	A–B	
Lesson 2: Field Trip	C–F	
Lesson 3: Subtracting with Base-Ten Pieces	G–J	Parts 1–2
Lesson 4: Paper-and-Pencil Subtraction	K–N	
Lesson 5: Workshop: Subtraction	O–R	
Lesson 6: Leonardo the Traveler	S–T	Parts 3–4
Lesson 7: Addition and Subtraction: Practice and Estimation	U–V	
Lesson 8: Class Party	W–Z	Parts 5–6

Math Facts

Use the practice in this unit to review the subtraction facts in Groups 1–4 and to develop strategies for solving the last six multiplication facts (4×6, 4×7, 4×8, 6×7, 6×8, 7×8.)

Time to the Nearest Minute

Write the time shown on each clock. Give the time to the nearest minute.
Use your individual clocks to help you.

1.

_____

2.

_____

3.

_____

4.

_____

5.

_____

6.

_____

Subtraction Strategies

Jerome, Tanya, and Nila started working on the problem 65 – 28.
They had to stop for a tornado drill.

1. Solve: 65 – 28 = ☐

2. Jerome drew a number line. Finish Jerome's number line sketch.
Where will he land?

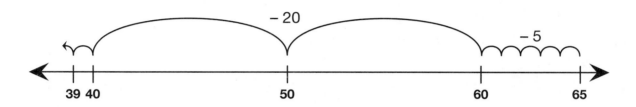

3. Tanya counted up from 28. She wrote these notes:

A. Fill in the circle and blanks to help Tanya finish.

$$28 + \textcircled{30} = 58$$
$$58 + \bigcirc = 65$$

So the answer is 30 + ___ = ___

B. Describe Tanya's strategy in words.

4. Nila started subtracting 28 from 65 by using expanded form. Help Nila finish subtracting.

$$65 \ = \ 60 + 5 \ = \ 50 + \underline{}$$
$$\underline{28} \ = \ \underline{20 + 8} \ = \ \underline{20 + \ \ 8 }$$
$$30 + \underline{} \ = \ \underline{}$$

5. Solve 72 – 47 using Jerome's, Tanya's, or Nila's strategy. Explain your thinking.

 Check-In: Questions 6–7

6. Solve the problems below using mental math, sketching a number line, or making a few quick notes.

A. 23 – 8 = ☐

B. 230 – 80 = ☐

C. 78 – 40 = ☐

D. 200 – 150 = ☐

E. 200 – 25 = ☐

F. 205 – 197 = ☐

G. 86 – 48 = ☐

H. 57 – 29 = ☐

7. Explain your strategy for Question 6F.

Solve the problems below by using mental math, sketching a number line, or making a few quick notes.

1. **A.** $17 - 8 =$ **B.** $47 - 8 =$

    C. $47 - 18 =$ **D.** $147 - 18 =$

    E. $170 - 80 =$ **F.** $175 - 80 =$

2. **A.** $100 - 51 =$ **B.** $100 - 76 =$

    C. $108 - 51 =$ **D.** $108 - 76 =$

    E. $200 - 51 =$ **F.** $200 - 76 =$

3. Explain how you solved the problem in Question 2D.

4. Explain how you solved the problem in Question 2E.

5. A. 364 – 98 =   **B.** 364 – 198 =

    C. 222 – 92 =   **D.** 222 – 192 =

6. Explain how you solved the problem in Question 5A.

7. A. 50 – 30 =   **B.** 50 – 29 =

    C. 79 – 28 =   **D.** 53 – 47 =

    E. 64 – 37 =   **F.** 71 – 38 =

8. Explain how you solved the problem in Question 7E.

Subtraction on Recording Sheets

1000s	100s	10s	1s

1000s	100s	10s	1s

1000s	100s	10s	1s

1000s	100s	10s	1s

1000s	100s	10s	1s

1000s	100s	10s	1s

Solve the following problems. Think of base-ten pieces as you record your trades.

1.

1000s	100s	10s	1s
		6	9
		− 2	5

2.

1000s	100s	10s	1s
		7	5
		− 3	8

3.

1000s	100s	10s	1s
	3	4	6
	− 2	2	8

4.

1000s	100s	10s	1s
	3	8	9
	− 1	9	1

5.

1000s	100s	10s	1s
	5	7	6
	− 3	8	9

6.

1000s	100s	10s	1s
6	3	2	5
− 4	8	1	6

Recording Your Subtraction

Nisha wanted to solve 423 – 319. She put out 4 flats, 2 skinnies, and 3 bits.

She realized she could not take
9 bits from 3 bits. So she traded
1 skinny for 10 bits. Then she
had 1 skinny and 13 bits.

1000s	100s	10s	1s
	4	2	3
–	3	1	9

1000s	100s	10s	1s
	4	$\cancel{2}$ ¹	$\cancel{3}$ ¹³
–	3	1	9

After the trade, she took away
9 bits. She also took away
1 skinny and 3 flats.

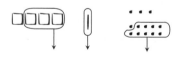

1000s	100s	10s	1s
	4	$\cancel{2}$ ¹	$\cancel{3}$ ¹³
–	3	1	9
	1	0	4

1. How did Nisha show that she traded one skinny for ten bits?

Name _____ Date _____

Solve the following problems. Think of base-ten pieces as you record your trades.

2.

1000s	100s	10s	1s
		3	9
		− 2	4

3.

1000s	100s	10s	1s
		7	3
		− 4	5

4.

1000s	100s	10s	1s
	4	5	2
	− 2	2	9

5.

1000s	100s	10s	1s
	6	7	8
	− 1	9	2

✔ Check-In: Questions 6–7

6.

1000s	100s	10s	1s
	8	4	6
	− 3	8	8

7.

1000s	100s	10s	1s
3	3	5	4
− 1	8	1	6

Johnny's Paper-and-Pencil Subtraction

Homework

1. Johnny solved a problem and recorded his work. Explain why he wrote the 2 above the 3 and the 15 above the 5.

$$
\begin{array}{r}
^{2\ 15}\!\!\!\!\!\!\!\!\! \\
7\,\cancel{3}\,\cancel{5} \\
-\ \ 1\,7\,8 \\
\hline
7
\end{array}
$$

2. Johnny continued the problem. Explain why he wrote 6 above the 7 and 12 above the 2.

$$
\begin{array}{r}
^{12} \\
^{6\ \cancel{2}\ 15} \\
\cancel{7}\,\cancel{3}\,\cancel{5} \\
-\ \ 1\,7\,8 \\
\hline
5\,5\,7
\end{array}
$$

Solve the problems.

3.

$$
\begin{array}{r}
687 \\
- 49 \\
\hline
\end{array}
$$

4.

$$
\begin{array}{r}
4327 \\
- 263 \\
\hline
\end{array}
$$

5.

$$
\begin{array}{r}
3067 \\
- 1478 \\
\hline
\end{array}
$$

6.

$$
\begin{array}{r}
2056 \\
- 1689 \\
\hline
\end{array}
$$

7.

$$
\begin{array}{r}
1003 \\
- 999 \\
\hline
\end{array}
$$

8.

$$
\begin{array}{r}
489 \\
- 301 \\
\hline
\end{array}
$$

9. Show a way to solve Question 7 in your head.

10. Show a way to solve Question 8 in your head.

Paper-and-Pencil Subtraction

Checking with Addition

1. Johnny solved a few subtraction problems but made some mistakes. Use addition to check his answers. If an answer is wrong, rewrite the problem and solve it correctly. Check with addition.

A.

```
    473
  - 205
    268
```

B.

```
   1489
  - 597
   1992
```

C.

```
   3232
  - 1581
   2751
```

D.

```
   6005
  - 2783
   3222
```

2. Solve the following problems. Show how to use addition to check your work.

A.

```
    343
  - 204
```

B.

```
   1379
  - 597
```

C.

```
   4141
  - 2690
```

D.

```
   4007
  - 3873
```

Name _____

Date _____

Subtraction Strategies Menu

Finding Friendly Numbers

428 − 179

430 − 200 = 230

230 is a reasonable estimate.

Kim

Counting Up

300 − 198 = 102

198 + ② = 200
200 + ⑩⑩ = 300

100 + 2 = 102

Luis

Counting Back

488 − 199 = 289

+1   −100   −100
288 289   388   488

488 − 100 − 100 + 1 = 289

Sam

Using Base-Ten Pieces

628 − 416 = 212

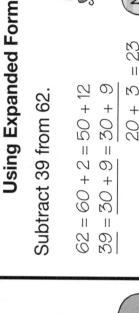

200 + 10 + 2 = 212

Carla

Using Expanded Form

Subtract 39 from 62.

$62 = 60 + 2 = 50 + 12$
$39 = 30 + 9 = 30 + 9$

$20 + 3 = 23$

Natasha

Using the Compact Method

$$\begin{array}{r} {}^{11} \\ 3\,{}^{1}\!\!\!\!\cancel{4}\,{}^{13} \\ \cancel{4}\cancel{2}\cancel{3} \\ -\ 1\,6\,5 \\ \hline 2\,5\,8 \end{array}$$

Frank

Largest to Smallest Game

The object of the game is to be the first player to reach 1000. This game is for two to four players.

Materials

- 0–6 spinner
- clear plastic spinner or a pencil and paper clip
- paper

Directions

On your turn,

1. Spin the spinner three times and use the numbers to make the largest three-digit number possible. Write this number on a sheet of paper.

2. Spin the spinner again three times and use these numbers to make the smallest three-digit number possible. Write this number on a sheet of paper. If this second number is larger than the first, spin again.

3. Subtract the smaller number from the larger number. The answer is your score for the round.

4. Add the score from this round to your scores from the other rounds. The first player to reach 1000 is the winner.

Round 1	Round 2	Score	Round 3	Score
504	632	271	310	847
− 233	− 56	+ 576	− 146	+ 164
271	576	847	164	1011

Variation

Change the winning goal or the size of the numbers. For example, spin to make four-digit numbers and try to reach the sum of 10,000.

Strategies to Subtract

Using Base-Ten Pieces

 **Self-Check: Question 1**

1. Solve 243 – 163 using base-ten pieces. Record your work with base-ten shorthand and the recording sheet.

1000s	100s	10s	1s	Number Sentences

Use the Workshop Menu below to choose practice with using base-ten pieces to subtract.

Workshop Menu			
	▲ **Working On It!**	● **Getting It!**	■ **Got It!**
Can I Do This?	I could use some extra help. *Lee Yah*	I just need some more practice. *Roberto*	I'm ready for a challenge. *Michael*
Use the base-ten pieces to subtract.	**Questions 2–4, 8–9**	**Questions 4–9**	**Questions 4, 6–9**

Solve using base-ten pieces. Record your work with base-ten shorthand and the recording sheet.

▲▢▢ **2.** 98 − 54

1000s	100s	10s	1s	Number Sentences

▲▢▢ **3.**
$$\begin{array}{r} 62 \\ -\ 28 \\ \hline \end{array}$$

1000s	100s	10s	1s	Number Sentences

▲●■ **4.**
$$\begin{array}{r} 154 \\ -\ 28 \\ \hline \end{array}$$

1000s	100s	10s	1s	Number Sentences

Workshop: Subtraction

Name _____   Date _____

5. 2445
    − 1238

1000s	100s	10s	1s	Number Sentences

6. 1456
    − 388

1000s	100s	10s	1s	Number Sentences

7. 2486 − 1587

1000s	100s	10s	1s	Number Sentences

▲●■ 8. Look at Tara's solution to 354 − 168.

$$354 = 300 + 50 + 4 = 200 + 140 + 14$$
$$\underline{168 = 100 + 60 + 8} = \underline{100 + 60 + 8}$$
$$ 100 + 80 + 6 = 186$$

This is a lot like using base-ten pieces or shorthand.

Tara

A. Show how to solve 354 − 168 with base-ten shorthand and a base-ten recording sheet.

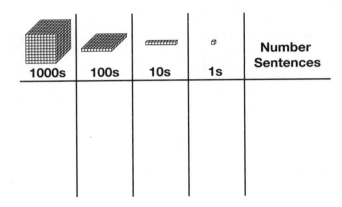

1000s	100s	10s	1s	**Number Sentences**

B. Do you agree with Tara? Why or why not?

▲●■ 9. Choose problems from Questions 1–7 to solve using expanded form. Show your work below.

Using Mental Math Strategies

✓ Self-Check: Questions 10–11

10. Use a mental math strategy to solve 205 – 75. Explain your strategy.

11. Use a number line to show how to solve 326 – 27.

Use the Workshop Menu to choose practice with using mental math strategies to subtract.

Workshop Menu			
Can I Do This?	▲ **Working On It!** I could use some extra help. *Roberto*	● **Getting It!** I just need some more practice. *Michael*	■ **Got It!** I'm ready for a challenge. *Lee Yah*
Use mental math strategies to subtract.	**Questions 12–14, 15E–G**	**Questions 13–15**	**Questions 14–15**

▲ ☐ ☐ 12. Mrs. Hunter challenged the class to use a mental math strategy to solve each of the problems below. Grace and her classmates recorded their mental math strategies. Solve the problem next to each one using a similar strategy. Explain your thinking to your partner.

 341 − 99 =

"99 is close to 100.
341 − 100 = 241. I took away 1 too many, so I added it back in.
241 + 1 = 242."

Grace

A. 132 − 98 =

157 − 25 =

"I thought about money."

150 − 25 = 125 + 7 = 132

Peter

B. 504 − 175 =

328 − 50 =

"I made notes, but I pictured the number line and counted back. I started at 328, hopped +2 to 330. Then − 10 five times and landed on 280. Then I hopped +2 to 278."

Ana

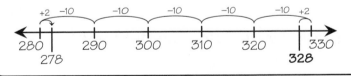

C. 352 − 98 =

220 − 160 =

"I counted up."

160 + (40) = 200
200 + (20) = 220
40 + 20 = 60

Frank

D. 320 − 250 =

▲●□ **13.** Use a mental math strategy to solve 1400 – 1198. Explain your strategy to your partner. Make some notes to record your partner's strategy below. Include your partner's name.

▲●■ **14.** Use a mental math strategy to solve 756 – 75. Explain your strategy to your partner. Make some notes to record your partner's strategy below. Include your partner's name.

15. Solve the following problems using a mental math strategy. Record your answer and explain your strategy to your partner. You do **not** need to write your strategy down, but you can jot down some notes.

◻|●|■ **A.** 350 − 125 =   ◻|●|■ **B.** 604 − 498 =

◻|●|■ **C.** 997 − 203 =   ◻|●|■ **D.** 825 − 427 =

▲|●|■ **E.** 747 − 297 =   ▲|●|■ **F.** 1002 − 997 =

▲|●|■ **G.** Show how you solved one of the problems above by describing your strategy in the thought bubble below.

Using Different Methods

 Self-Check: Question 16

Use the *Subtraction Strategies Menu* in the *Student Guide* Reference section.

16. Solve 43 – 27 using three different strategies or methods.

Use the Workshop menu to choose practice with subtraction methods.

Workshop Menu			
	▲ **Working On It!**	● **Getting It!**	■ **Got It!**
Can I Do This?	I could use some extra help. Nicholas	I just need some more practice. Jacob	I'm ready for a challenge. Ana
Use different methods to subtract.	**Questions 17–20** **Use each of these methods at least once:** • base-ten pieces • expanded form	**Questions 20–21** **Use each of these methods at least once:** • base-ten pieces • expanded form • compact method	**Questions 20–21** **Use each of these methods at least once:** • expanded form • compact method

▲□□ **17.** Here is how Sam solved
235 − 126.

	100s	10s	1s
	2	3	5
	2	2	15
− 1	1	2	6
	1	0	9

Use the same method to solve
353 − 235.

	100s	10s	1s

▲□□ **18.** Here is how Maya solved
364 − 247.

364 = 300 + 60 + 4 = 300 + 50 + 14
247 = 200 + 40 + 7 = 200 + 40 + 7
                           100 + 10 + 7
                         = 117

Use the same method to solve
327 − 172.

▲□□ **19.** Here is how Josh solved
476 − 329.

$$\begin{array}{r} {}^{6\ 16}\\ 476 \\ + 329 \\ \hline 147 \end{array}$$

Use the same method to solve
847 − 278.

▲●■ **20.** Choose your own strategies and methods to solve the following
problems. Use the *Subtraction Strategies Menu*.

A. 137 – 68

B. 166
     – 46

C. 542 – 474

D. 446 – 210

E. 232 – 124

F. 7442
     – 3256

G. 202
     – 150

H. 2551 – 1450

21. • Using the *Subtraction Strategies Menu* as a guide, show how to solve each problem using two different strategies. Compare your strategies. Circle the one you like best.

• Use a mental math strategy at least three times.

• Use each paper-and-pencil strategy at least once.

One Strategy	Another Strategy
A. $427 - 325 =$	
B. $400 - 298 =$	
C. $\begin{array}{r} 675 \\ -\ 598 \\ \hline \end{array}$	
D. $\begin{array}{r} 460 \\ -\ 356 \\ \hline \end{array}$	

Did you try all of the strategies on the *Subtraction Strategies Menu*?

Helping Leonardo the Traveler Solve Problems

In the beginning of the story, Leonardo learned to use the abacus. Use the pictures below to show numbers the way Leonardo's father taught him.

1. A. Draw pebbles on the abacus to show 680.

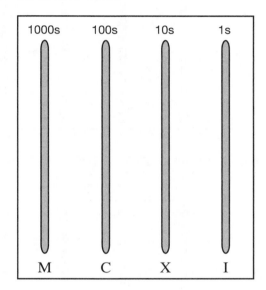

B. Draw pebbles on the abacus to show 1905.

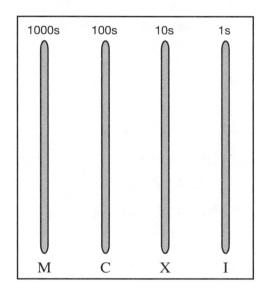

C. Use base-ten shorthand to show each of these numbers. Use the Fewest Pieces Rule.

680

1905

Complete the questions. Use the *Addition Strategies Menu* and the *Subtraction Strategies Menu* in the Referece section when needed.

2. A. What two numbers are shown on the abacus?

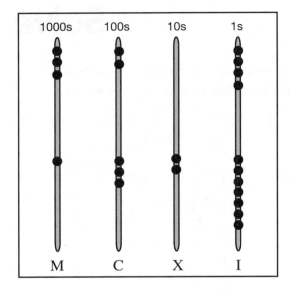

B. Add these two numbers together using the compact method.

3. The Arab teacher, Ali, showed Leonardo how to combine the two numbers shown on the abacus.

A. What number is shown on the top part of the abacus?

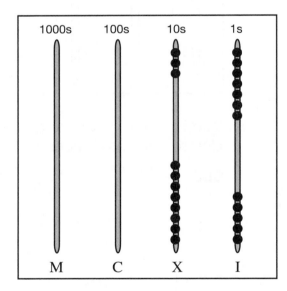

B. What number is shown on the bottom part of the abacus?

C. Show Leonardo how to add the numbers shown on the abacus using expanded form and a number line.

4. A. The problem that Ali showed Leonardo is below. Help Leonardo
finish the problem.

$$\overset{1}{3}7$$
$$\underline{+\ 85}$$
$$2$$

B. What does the little one above the 3 stand for?

5. Help Leonardo solve the problem using the
compact method. Think of base-ten pieces
and show your trades.

6. Look at the abacus that Leonardo used to show 95 in the problem 95 – 37.

   A. How many tens and how many ones does the abacus show?

   B. Write a number sentence for what the abacus shows.

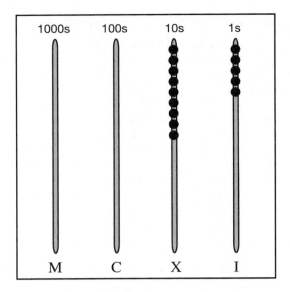

7. Look at the way Leonardo made trades on the abacus.

   A. How many tens and how many ones does the abacus show now?

   B. Does the abacus still show a number that is equal to 95? Tell how you know.

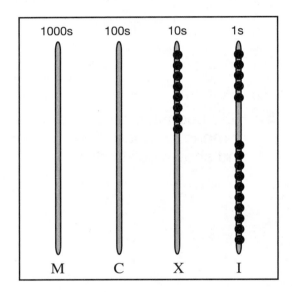

   C. Write a number sentence for what the abacus shows.

   D. Show Leonardo how to use counting up to solve 95 – 37.

8. Leonardo and Omar solved this problem.

A. What does the 7 above the 8 stand for?

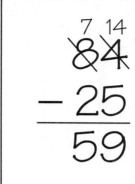

B. What does the 14 above the 4 stand for?

C. Complete the number sentence below to show 84 after trades are made.

70 + _____ = 84

D. Omar wrote the number sentence 7 + 14 = 84.

Do you agree with Omar? Why or why not?

E. Show Leonardo how to use expanded form to solve 84 − 25.

9. Show Leonardo how to solve 275 − 196 = _____ using counting back on a number line.

10. A. Draw pebbles on the abacus to show 42.

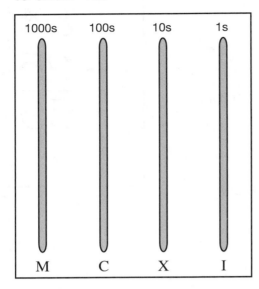

Number sentence:

_____

B. Draw pebbles on the abacus to show 42 another way.

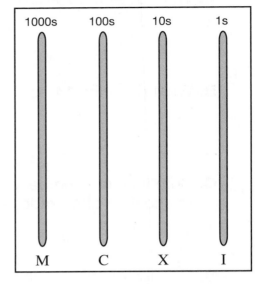

Number sentence:

_____

C. Use the abacus to show 42 – 17.

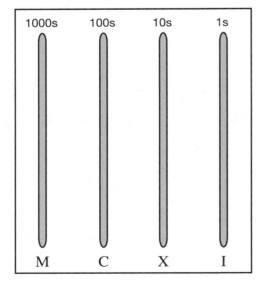

Number sentence:

_____

D. Solve 42 – 17 using expanded form.

E. Compare the abacus strategy to the expanded form. How are they similar?

Name _____ Date _____

Helping Leonardo the Traveler Solve Problems Feedback Box	Expectation	Check In	Comments
Apply place value concepts to make connections among representations of numbers to the thousands using base-ten pieces and number lines. (Q# 1–10)	E8		
Represent and solve subtraction problems using base-ten pieces and number lines. (Q# 5, 6, 9)	E2		
Subtract multidigit numbers using mental math strategies (e.g., composing and decomposing numbers and counting up). (Q# 7, 9)	E3		
Subtract multidigit numbers using paper-and-pencil methods (e.g., expanded form, and compact). (Q# 5, 8, 10)	E4		

Workspace

Workspace

Workspace

Workspace

Workspace

Workspace

Workspace

Workspace

Workspace

Workspace

Workspace